Mission Miracles

Mission Miracles

Eileen Lantry
with David and Becky Gates

Pacific Press® Publishing Association
Nampa, Idaho
Oshawa, Ontario, Canada
www.pacificpress.com

Cover design by Eucaris L. Galicia
Inside design by Bruce A. Fenner
Photos provided by David Gates

Copyright © 2007 by
Pacific Press® Publishing Association
Printed in the United States of America
All rights reserved

Additional copies of this book may be obtained
by calling toll-free 1-800-765-6955
or online at http://www.adventistbookcenter.com.

Unless otherwise noted, all Scripture quotations are from the New King
James Version of the Bible, © copyright 1979, 1980, 1982,
by Thomas Nelson, Inc., Publishers.

ISBN 13: 978-0-8163-2186-5
ISBN 10: 0-8163-2186-8

07 08 09 10 · 5 4 3 2 1

Contents

CHAPTER 1

Volunteers Are Special People

Nothing disturbed Jodi's sleep. Not the insects chirping, not the owls hooting, not the sounds of distant cattle moving about in the night. Not even the ever-present bats, chattering and arguing in the open rafters above her bedroom. Exhausted by a long day of teaching, she didn't hear the occasional crash of mangoes and coconuts falling on the tin roofs of homes across the river. She didn't hear the "song" of the frogs that filled the forest with a noise like chainsaws revving up their engines. Jodi McDaniels slept quietly after a strenuous day of dealing with sixty students at Kimbia Mission Academy beside the Berbice River in Guyana, South America.

Her husband, Warren, the school administrator, had gone to Georgetown, the capitol of the country, and would be returning soon with Melissa and Gilbert Sissons, who would be leading out in medical work up and down the river. The Sissons were not new to the area. Gilbert and Melissa, both graduates of Loma Linda University, started mission work in Guyana in July 2001. Though Gilbert has a master's degree in speech-language pathology, he had spent three years helping with construction projects and studying the Bible with the local people in Guyana. He helped construct the main school building on campus. Melissa served as the nurse for both the school and the community. Like the McDanielses, Gilbert and Melissa Sissons are volunteer mission workers.

Suddenly, high-pitched screams cut through the jungle sounds and caused Jodi to sit straight up in bed. Girls were screaming somewhere outside, and over the screams of the girls, she thought she could hear a baby crying. Quickly, she jumped out of bed and started running toward the commotion.

At the same time David Hossick also heard the screams and woke up. An ADRA volunteer, David spends three months a year in Guyana doing all types of maintenance. His first thought was that someone had been bitten by a snake. He leaped out of bed and down the stairs, ready to help. As he reached the corner of the building, he met Jodi running full speed. David joined her.

The night was pitch black; no moon cast its glow. By now the entire campus had awakened. Even the villagers across the river heard the pandemonium. Near the pit toilet, Jodi and Dave met a group of hysterical girls, all yelling. "It's Julita. She's had a baby—and it fell into the toilet!"

Sure enough, they heard an infant's piercing cry from the muck beneath. There was no time to try to sort out what had happened. First, the baby must be rescued immediately from the six-foot abyss. And the young mother needed help.

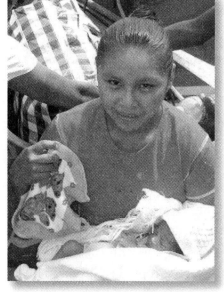

Julita and her baby. The circumstances surrounding the birth caused quite a bit of excitement.

Julita had come to Kimbia Mission Academy from Kopinang, a mountainous village west of the Berbice River region. Fifteen years old, she was barely four feel tall and had the classic Amerindian petite frame. Julita was a wonderful student with an addictive, bubbly giggle. Yet, she was quiet and shy—never one to push herself forward. Quietly and bravely, she concealed her developing pregnancy, never asking for help, never complaining, and never telling the nurse or any faculty member of her condition.

The day she went into labor, she had worked hard in the school garden, digging irrigation trenches as diligently as her male classmates. That night she cried into her pillow in her bunk bed in the dorm until someone heard her and called the girls' dean. Assuming Julita suffered from gas pains, the dean went to boil her some tea. Julita did not want tea. Instead, she got out of bed and walked with some friends through the inky darkness to the toilet. As they stood outside the stall, the girls could hear her moaning. Then they heard a final groan, a heavy splash, and the cry of a newborn baby. Julita had delivered her child!

"Julita," they screamed, "what is going on? Is that a baby crying? Tell us, Julita, what happened?"

"I don't know; I don't know," Julita mumbled in confusion.

When David and Jodi arrived, David's mind instantly went into high gear. He'd faced a lot of things in his years of mission work, but he realized that it would take divine intervention this time for a life not to be lost. He began shouting in his excitement, "God, please help us to save this baby!" Then he turned and commanded, "Get me a chain saw—quick! And two rakes to scoop up the baby! Hurry! Hurry!"

He heard Jodi crying, "Lord, help us! Lord, help us!"

Then he beamed his flashlight down deep into the hole of the toilet and saw a tiny infant lying on its back, crying. "Praise the Lord!" he exclaimed. "It's on its back. The umbilical cord snapped during the fall."

Jodi held the light while David maneuvered the two rakes down and around the infant's body. Unfortunately they were cheap rakes, and the heads of each had broken in half—opposite halves. This made it much more difficult for David, but slowly, carefully, he began to bring the baby to the top. As he worked, Jodi shouted orders

The outhouse at Kimbia Mission Academy in Guyana where Julita's baby was born—and nearly died.

left and right. "Get hot water! Get towels! Someone get Pearl, the health worker!" Another person ran to get clean clothes. Everything seemed utter chaos. Numerous prayers continued to ascend to God.

At last the baby was right near the top of the hole. But Jodi and David couldn't reach the infant because of the angle of the rake handles. In horror they watched the slippery little body slide away and plunge back into the darkness—face down!

Devastated, Jodi cried out, "If we can't get that baby in the next minute, I'm jumping down inside there myself."

"Let's give it one more try," David urged. At the same time he yelled, "Start up the chain saw in case we have to cut open the toilet and dive in. In what seemed like an eternity, they slowly brought the baby up again with the rakes. This time Jodi grabbed it and held it securely, ignoring the smelly muck that covered its body.

From birth to rescue, the whole incident took less than ten minutes, thanks to God and the angels. Jodi swaddled the infant, a baby girl, and rushed it to her home to clean off the sewage. The health worker arrived and attended to a shaken and traumatized young mother. She clamped the cord and cut it. With the health worker's assistance, Julita finished the delivery of her placenta.

No one slept the rest of that night. Many stared blankly into the moonless sky. What had happened? How would this change life on Kimbia Mission Academy campus? What would become of Julita and her new little daughter?

Later, when volunteer nurse Melissa Sissons arrived on campus, the baby and mother received a full assessment. Amazingly, not one complication could be found. The baby weighed three and a half pounds and was seventeen inches long. She had a full head of black hair and had no trouble learning to breast feed.

Construction goes forward on the school buildings at Kimbia Mission Academy as local individuals work with student missionaries from the United States to complete the needed facilities.

Melissa Sissons took young Julita and baby to the Georgetown Hospital. Eventually Gary Roberts, a volunteer pilot for Guyana Adventist Medical Aviation Service (GAMAS), flew her back to her home village. The staff and students continually pray that Julita will stay close to God who loves her and her baby and that He will give her wisdom as she starts a new and challenging life in her village. What a wonderful God we serve! He is a God who is always with us to deliver us from the muck and mire of this sinful world.

The story of Julita and the miraculous rescue of her baby is just one of the thousands of miracles David and Becky Gates have witnessed since they gave their lives to God in volunteer mission service. In 1996, David, Becky, and their five children landed in Kaikan, Guyana, ready to serve. And God has continually answered their prayers with miraculous evidences of His care and leading. Back then, the entire village of Kaikan, all 150 villagers, met the new missionaries at the airstrip. Today, this dedicated couple still rejoice that they can work as volunteer missionaries, without a salary, trusting God completely, and accepting His abundant miracles of grace. And He has blessed their work far beyond anything they imagined at the beginning.

During those early years, David, a licensed pilot, established the Guyana Adventist Medical Aviation Service (GAMAS) to carry on medical evangelistic work in the remote jungle villages of Guyana. Lives were saved—both physically and spiritually. "I'm so glad we chose to step out in faith, depending wholly on God," Becky recalls. "He supplied the needs of His precious Amerindian children. God more than kept His promises. Not only did

A person needing medical attention is carried to a waiting GAMAS airplane. The Guyana Adventist Medical Aviation Service saves lives physically and spiritually in remote areas of the country.

He provide for all our needs—and theirs—but His blessings enabled us to introduce them to a God they didn't know."

When God provided another airplane, David begin looking for an experienced, willing volunteer pilot to help him cope with the urgent calls GAMAS was receiving. That is when he came in contact with Gary Roberts—a meeting that David considers anything but coincidence.

Born in East Africa, Gary spent the first fourteen years of his life in Zaire, now the Democratic Republic of Congo, where his parents were missionaries. He helped his mother, a nurse, in the medical clinic and flew in the small mission airplane with his dad, who was a pilot and mechanic. Gary grew up speaking four languages—English, French, Swahili, and a difficult tribal dialect of the local area. When he turned fifteen, his family moved to Indonesia, where he learned a fifth language—and obtained his pilot's license.

While Gary was in college at Southern Adventist University, taking nursing and working at the Collegedale airport doing airplane maintenance, David came in contact with this young man. Both are convinced that the meeting was God's doing.

"During my freshman year in college," Gary recalls, "I was praying for God to lead me into an opportunity to serve as a mission pilot and nurse." When he met David and learned of the need for just such a person in Guyana, he told David that he would be ready for the job as soon as he graduated from college.

During Gary's senior year, David invited him to take part in a jungle survival course to be held in Peru the last three weeks of Gary's final semester in college. The university rules for nursing students stated that any student missing more than two days of classes would be automatically dismissed. Gary prayed about the situation. Then he wrote the faculty a letter explaining that he intended to join GAMAS after graduation to serve the Amerindians in unentered regions of Guyana's interior. He pointed out how the jungle survival course would be vital to his plans. His dedication and pleas—along with the influence of the Holy Spirit—impressed the nursing faculty to grant his request.

Wendy, Gary's fiancée, shared his dream and his dedication. Together they pledged themselves to be willing volunteer missionaries, trusting God completely. David was thrilled when he learned that the university had given Gary permission to attend the jungle survival course in Peru. But Gary didn't have the money for airfare to South America. He told Wendy, "If God wants me to go, He'll supply the airfare."

During the Christmas break of 2000–2001, Gary and Wendy flew to the Northwest to visit his grandparents. As they waited for their flight, they heard the announcement, "This flight is overbooked. If anyone is willing to give up his seat and take a later flight, the airline will give that person two thousand dollars in airline vouchers." God had provided the means to pay for not one, but two, round trips to Guyana—another mission miracle!

Gary joined the GAMAS team in July 2001, while Wendy stayed in the United States to work off student loans and wait until Gary became established in Guyana. Then, after getting married in the States, they both would return to South America.

When Gary arrived in Guyana, David arranged to spend several weeks flying with him. "The authorities here require that new pilots have at least three hundred hours of jungle flying in the country before they receive permission to fly alone," David told Gary. "But because of your flying in Indonesia, I'm sure they'll waive that requirement. We'll know in two months."

In Georgetown, Gary stayed in a small apartment. He was usually out of bed by 4:00 A.M. so he could get to the airport, load and fuel the plane, and be in the air by sunrise. Then he flew all day until sunset. For about a year he worked in Guyana without Wendy. He determined he would never bring her to live in the apartment where he was staying; so, in his spare time, which wasn't often, he looked for a place to rent. He couldn't find anything suitable. Eventually, he worked out a deal with Davis Memorial Adventist Hospital in Georgetown to stay for a while in one of its small apartments. He would have preferred not living in Georgetown at all but in the interior. But he knew that someone had to live in the capital in order to purchase supplies, host volunteers, and care for all the government paperwork and permissions that required ongoing attention.

In July 2002, Gary flew back to Collegedale, Tennessee, for a simple, but beautiful, wedding ceremony. For Wendy, who had been an active ICU nurse, living in Guyana meant losing much of her independence. Drivers in Guyana seemed erratic and frightening to her—plus they drove on the left side of the road! It wasn't safe for her to walk alone or even to take a taxi by herself. With Gary flying all day, she was alone much of the time. One day, returning late, he called her on the radio, saying, "What do you need at the market? Since it's late, I'll stop by on the way home."

"Please!" Wendy was almost in tears. "I've been looking forward to getting out of this apartment for four days. And today is the day for fresh fruit and vegetables in the market. Please come get me!"

Gary and Wendy Roberts have dedicated their lives to volunteer mission service. They witness God's miracles on a daily basis.

Slowly, however, Wendy began to regain control of her life. She made herself learn to drive amid the chaos of Georgetown traffic. With Jeremiah 42:3 on her lips—"Show us the way in which we should walk and the thing we should do"—she ventured out to find activities and areas where she felt safe. Wendy found that nothing was easy in Guyana compared to what she was used to. Even shopping for groceries was complicated. After she found the items she wanted to purchase, she would have to take them to a worker who would write up the bill. Then she needed to go to the cashier to pay. Next, she would take her purchases to a third location in the store to be checked and stamped as paid. Finally, she would stop at the door for her receipt before being able to leave the store. And since most shops sold only special items—not a wide variety—this process had to be repeated again and again in different stores. All this absorbed huge amounts of Wendy's time. But she continued depending on God for strength and power, growing more confident and experienced. And soon she was purchasing supplies for twenty North American volunteer workers at the Davis Indian Industrial College in Paruima and Kimbia Academy and for twenty-five Bible workers in eight villages. Gary delivered the supplies by plane and picked up mail.

Wendy and Gary found that Jesus was beside them as they dedicated themselves to His service. Mission miracles? They experience them on a daily basis.

Chapter 2

God Builds a School

David and Becky Gates felt that God's plans for Guyana included the many children who had never had an opportunity to receive a Christian education and learn about Jesus. They had a dream of an Adventist academy in Guyana. This is the story of how God worked to make that dream a reality.

As David and Becky developed plans for an academy in the Kimbia area of Guyana, students and faculty members at Laurelbrook Academy in Tennessee decided to help; a group from the school would go to Guyana in January 2001 and start the construction from scratch—digging and pouring the footings for the first building. One of the students, David Parnell, invited his older brother, Warren, to join him and his classmates on the mission trip.

God had recently impressed Warren with a desire to serve Him more fully than his current involvement in corporate America allowed. So, Warren arranged to take three weeks of his vacation time and join ten Laurelbrook students and three faculty members on the mission project.

The mission team arrived in Kimbia after dark. The boys stayed in one "lamb shelter" (a building outside the church where Sabbath School classes met), and the girls in the other. They began work the next morning. Except for Sabbath, their schedule was the same each day—arise at 6:00 A.M., eat breakfast and have worship, followed by a five minute trip across the river to the work site. Mornings were spent digging trenches for footings, straightening rebar and placing it in the trenches, mixing and pouring concrete one wheelbarrow load at a time, and laying blocks. A total of six courses of block laid the foundation for the one hundred foot by thirty foot main school building. Noon found them back across the river for lunch and a short rest through the hottest part of the day. Work began again at 2:00 P.M. and continued until 5:00. Supper and evening worship followed, and since the sun sets around 6:00

The generosity of this couple, who donated the property for Kimbia Mission Academy to be built, and the dedicated efforts of the initial building committee made the school possible.

P.M. every day in the tropics and since there was no electricity on the site and since everyone was tired anyway, sleep came quickly and soundly. This simple life appealed to Warren.

The McDaniels family—Jodi, Warren, Warren III, and Taylor. Their desire to serve God more fully led them to leave the United States for service at Kimbia Mission Academy.

On his way back to the United States, Warren called his wife, Jodi. "Would you consider moving to Guyana? I have an opportunity to be principal of the new school in Kimbia by the Berbice River. Leading the school and teaching young people is a more appealing challenge than making money in America. I'd like to close out our electrical engineering business and work totally for God. Would you be willing to sell our houses and cars and come work as a volunteer missionary, developing a school in what is now mostly jungle?"

Jodi agreed, and so on November 6, 2001, Warren and Jodi McDaniels, along with their children—nine-year-old daughter, Taylor, and six-year-old son, Warren III—arrived in the jungle of Guyana.

Construction on the administration building of Kimbia Mission Academy continued through January and February 2002. The academy opened for classes in March as a day school with twenty-seven students. The lower level of the building consisted of an open expanse of mud. Living, eating, and classes all took place in the upstairs level for the first three months.

Then the Laurelbrook Academy group came again from Tennessee to pour a concrete floor in the lower level and build classroom partitions throughout the building. Knowing how long it takes for materials to make their way seventy-five miles up the Berbice River, Warren had ordered thirty-nine tons of gravel many weeks before the Laurelbrook group arrived to begin work. Only nineteen tons arrived. Each day the volunteers

Work progresses on the initial school building at Kimbia Mission Academy. Here God performed a miracle with gravel!

mixed the gravel with sand and cement to pour the floor. The pile of gravel began to diminish markedly. Finally the day came when the workers calculated there was just enough gravel for "one more pour." Just as they finished pouring this one last section, rain began falling. That put a stop to the concrete work for the day. They spent their time building wooden partitions, dividing the new floor into classrooms and hallways.

The next day the workers looked once more at the gravel pile. "It looks like there is still enough gravel for another pour," they said to one another. So, they began mixing a batch of concrete—and, yes, there was just enough gravel. They poured the concrete and had just completed smoothing it when the rain began. They went back to working inside as they had the day before.

The next day the same thing happened! And the next day. And the next. Day after day, there always continued to be just enough gravel for one more batch of concrete! And just as that pour was completed, the rain would come to end concrete work for that day. The workers praised God, remembering Elijah and the widow's never-failing jar of oil (see 1 Kings 17:9–16). That gravel pile became holy ground as God continued to multiply the original nineteen tons. When the Laurelbrook mission group departed for home, there was only one room in the building left without a concrete floor—and there was still enough gravel left for "one more pour"! Truly a "mission miracle."

Does God supply our needs? Just ask the students and teachers of Laurelbrook. They'll answer with a resounding "Yes, we saw a daily miracle!"

With the construction of the new school building, the staff and students of Kimbia could now spread out. Classes could move downstairs, and student missionaries who had been housed across the river in the Sabbath School buildings could move into the upstairs rooms next to the McDanielses' living quarters. Things were looking up!

During early months on the Berbice River, Jodi found that her biggest challenge was the outhouse, containing four separate stalls. Each stall was unique in size, shape, and efficiency of door closure! For Jodi, Warren, and the children, this resulted in a morning race for the "favorite" stall. One morning, young Warren won the race and triumphantly locked the door, laughing. But moments later his parents heard him scream, "Snake! Snake! He began beating on the door, trying to get out. But the door stuck and refused to budge.

Jodi and Warren frantically pulled on the door from the outside while the boy screamed and threw his weight against it from the inside. Suddenly the door flew open, and a very frightened boy tumbled out. Just a few feet overhead bobbed the head of a large snake coiled in the rafters at the back of the stall. Hearing the screams, Gilbert Sissons came on the run. Together he and Warren managed to kill the monstrous reptile. Stretched on the ground, the snake measured six feet long. Another mission miracle? Young Warren knows God sent His angel to "encamp" around him (see Psalm 34:7).

When the spring semester of 2002 closed, Warren and Jodi made it clear to the parents and students that school would not reopen until a girls' dormitory was completed. No longer would Kimbia Academy be a day school; it would become a boarding school. The surrounding communities agreed to contribute a share of labor and wood for the construction of the new dormitory. Yet, as the months came and went, no signs of progress could be seen.

The McDanielses had set aside money from the home they sold in the United States, hoping to build a modest home on the campus. What a relief it would be to move from the cramped quarters of four people living in a single room on the upper floor of the main school building! However, the amount of money it would take to build a home was just about the same amount that was needed to complete the dorm project. After struggling with the decision for a while, Warren and Jodi decided that the need for a girls' dormitory was greater than their need for a house. So, they willingly surrendered their "house money" and bought the necessary building materials. God honored their gift of love, and the Holy Spirit stepped in to change the attitudes of the local people—something that human effort alone could not have accomplished.

Classroom scenes at Kimbia Mission Academy. Students take a test, and principal Warren McDaniels teaches a class.

When the McDanielses gave up their dream for a house to buy the materials for a girls' dormitory, the community was convinced that Warren and Jodi meant what they said when they declared, "No dorm, no school." In August 2002 the local people came together to work with the staff in constructing a dormitory. "You've never seen a building go up so fast in your life," Jodi exclaims. "The people really worked!" Students, staff, and people from the community joined their efforts. Thirty days after the first post was set, the girls moved into their dorm, and classes began.

The building was not totally finished when school began; so, classes and construction continued side by side. Students worked two hours each day, along with the teachers, learning practical skills of construction, maintenance, plastering, and painting. They even poured concrete for sidewalks. God impressed individuals in the United States to send gifts to help purchase supplies. In the end, total building costs were only eight thousand U.S. dollars.

What about the McDanielses' dream of a home of their own? Gilbert and Melissa Sissons, who first arrived in Kimbia in August 2001, wrote to their friend, Mel Brass, a member of their home church in Ukiah, California. Mel told the church, "I can't feel comfortable living in a nice home while the McDaniels family is crowded into a single small room. Let's build two houses on the Kimbia Mission Academy campus—one for the principal's family and another for the permanent volunteer staff." The Ukiah church agreed.

Mel personally drew up plans for the two homes and then shipped a container to Guyana, filled with plumbing fixtures, sliding doors, exterior and interior doors, solar panels—everything needed to build two comfortable homes except the lumber, which could be better obtained locally.

Jodi and Warren were overwhelmed! God's providence convinced them more than anything else that He had truly led them in their decision to sell everything and dedicate themselves to full-time work in Guyana. Mission miracles? Definitely. What an awesome affirmation that God is the Master Builder at Kimbia Mission Academy.

About this time the Kimbia area experienced a severe drought for many months. The students told Jodi, "Teacher, soon you will be drinking river water."

"No," she assured them, "God will send rain water to fill our water tanks."

The next morning the sun shone brightly with not a cloud in the sky. The students reported, "There is no water left in the tanks—not a drop."

Jodi answered, "I prayed for rain this morning, and it will come." During English class that morning, everyone suddenly heard the sound of heavy rain, which continued for hours, completely filling the water tanks. Then the weather cleared, and again there was no rain for months. The opposite occurs during the rainy season: The days dawn foggy but clear up by midmorning, and rain drenches the area by early afternoon. Soon two to three inches of water and mud cover the entire campus.

The river is the focal point of life in the jungle. It serves as a super-highway. Huge three-story tugboats push oversized barges of bauxite up and down the river. Without the river, the people would have no bath tub or laundry. On Sunday the girls from Kimbia Mission Academy bathe and wash clothes from sunrise to 10:00 A.M. Then the boys do their laundry and swim.

Unfortunately, for generations the local inhabitants have believed that river people live under the water and steal children. In school, the students learn the truth of God and His promises that are found in the Bible; they share with their parents what they have learned. But these fears and superstitions are hard to eradicate—even after a person becomes a church member.

When an old man, who ran a tiny shop across the river, died, the students were greatly afraid. They believed that "Uncle Benji" would haunt his family and friends for nine days after his death. That night, the girls panicked in the dark and crept to the room of the volunteer dean. "Miss Abby," they begged, "we're afraid!" The girls' dean spent much of the night reading Bible promises to the girls and singing songs of trust with them. Then tucking them back in bed, she promised to leave her door ajar so they would feel less frightened and could sleep. After some worships and vespers and a sermon Warren preached the following Sabbath, all of the girls returned to their own beds and began trusting in God's promise: " 'I will never leave you nor forsake you' " (Hebrews 13:5).

By 2005, Kimbia Mission Academy's campus contained seven major buildings surrounded by much natural beauty. All these buildings—the main administration building, the boys' and girls' dormitories, two homes for missionary families, a cafeteria/kitchen, and a clinic/science building—have been built by the staff, students, local community people, and mission groups. Breathtaking sunrises and sunsets; a wide variety of flowers, birds, and animals; and startlingly bright, starry-night skies lead the students' thoughts to their great Creator, Redeemer, and Friend.

Students eat the midday meal in the school cafeteria.

God continually impresses dedicated people to join the growing group of volunteers who come to Guyana to shoulder heavy responsibilities. The number of volunteers has doubled almost every year. David and Becky Gates daily pray that God will continue to put His spirit of volunteering and sacrifice into the hearts of dedicated people while it is still possible to work freely. The success of the Gates' far-reaching mission program depends on adaptable, flexible administrators, teachers, pilots, mechanics, technicians, broadcasting specialists, construction workers, engineers, physicians, dentists, nurses, and others.

Some volunteers come for a short time, like Rilla (Toll) Klingbeil and her son, David, who volunteered to serve at the Davis Indian Industrial College (DIIC) in Paruima. Forty years earlier, Rilla had grown up in Paruima as a child of missionary parents. Her dream was to return and paint the rough-hewn boards of the existing buildings. With primer and paint, Rilla and David came not just for a visit but to paint the three two-story buildings on the campus. What a difference their gift of hard work and love made!

The graduates of the Davis Indian Bible Worker Training Program are some of the most self-sacrificing. Going out two by two, these new workers know isolation and hardship await them as they go forward with eager motivation to share the gospel. Yet, they are willing! And God continues to supply air support, food, materials for construction equipment, and evangelistic tools.

Sebastian and Ada Edmunds, along with Ray Hastings, all graduate Bible workers, had started sharing the gospel in the village of Kopinang

in an area of Guyana known as Region 8. This area is dominated by the Catholic Church, but by the power of the Holy Spirit, the workers had been able to lead many of the villagers to a new relationship with Jesus.

At this time, Sebastian and Ray went to their homes to spend some time with their families and to restock supplies for their

Sebastian and Ada Edmunds, trained as Bible workers at the Davis Indian Industrial College, shared the Adventist message with the people of Kopinang.

work in the village. After a week, they were eager to return to continue their ministry. They needed to construct a building that would serve as both a house and a church so they would have a place to live and also a church home for the new members.

David Gates flew Sebastian and Ray back to the village of Kopinang. David leveled the plane at nine thousand feet, and they flew for almost an hour. They could see a few mountaintops poking through the overcast. His instruments told David they were only a few miles from their destination near the Guyana-Brazil border. But he dared not descend through the cloud layer without clear visibility.

Above the noise of the engine, Sebastian shouted in David's ear, "The people in Kopinang seem so hungry to hear about Jesus. Most have never heard before that He's coming soon to take them home to heaven. I know God wants us to land safely." Then Sebastian prayed, "The mountains surround us, God, and we can't see to land! We need Your help, our faithful Chief!"

At that moment, David heard a voice on the radio. A friendly air taxi pilot flying nearby asked, "David, are you having trouble finding a way to descend? If you fly east toward the village from which I just left, you'll find the hole in the clouds you need to get underneath." Mission miracles! Does God care? Does He guide? Of course!

Smiling faces of children and adults surrounded the plane as the missionaries unloaded their supplies, including a new chain saw, fuel, oil, food, and materials to finish the construction of their new mission home-church. Being a nurse as well as a pilot, David examined and treated patients under the wing of the plane, while the Bible workers went about their duties.

David noticed the village priest standing nearby silently watching. He had never met the priest, so David stepped over and greeted him. He wanted to develop a friendly relationship with the priest, and he knew that medical ministry usually generates goodwill and opens doors. The priest had a kind, gentle look about him.

"Sir, would you please ask God's blessing on my flight back home?" David asked.

The priest's prayer surprised David, "Thank You, Father in heaven," he prayed. "Thank You for these good people. They've come to bring us better health and education for our children. Please accompany this pilot as he returns home."

What a thrill! thought David. *God has guided this man's attitude; the power of the Holy Spirit is beginning to open another village to the gospel.*

Meanwhile, in Georgetown, another volunteer couple was arriving from the United States about this time—Joe and Melody McWilliam. "Some Bible workers have begun sharing the Adventist message in the village of Kopinang in the interior of Guyana," Gary Roberts told them when they arrived in the country. "Would you be willing to go there for a few weeks to encourage the Bible workers? Then, when an opportunity opens up to bring the gospel to another village, you could transfer to that village and begin working there."

Joe and Melody agreed. They arrived in Kopinang in March 2002. Sebastian, Ada, and Ray welcomed them warmly. "About a year ago,

Joe and Melody McWilliam, volunteer missionaries in the village of Kopinang

we came to Kopinang," the three told Joe and Melody. "We had no place to live. Our first task was to make friends and prepare for a place to build. Gradually, we began sharing our faith. Now we are studying the Bible with fourteen people. Come and see our house-church combination. We live on the second floor, and the kitchen and church is below on the first floor. The building is twenty-six by thirty feet. We've finished the basic structure, but there is much yet to complete."

"We'll be glad to help any way we can," Joe and Melody assured them. And they pitched in willingly to help finish the building and to do anything else that was needed.

About a month after Joe and Melody arrived, the little group of volunteer missionaries rejoiced as twelve villagers were baptized. One couple, who had just been married, were baptized in their wedding clothes!

In June, when Gary Roberts returned to the United States to marry Wendy, David visited Kopinang and met Joe and Melody for the first time. "We're so thankful we volunteered to come to Guyana," they told him. They showed David the improvements that had been made in the time they had been in the village. "We've just finished putting in a new water project," Joe told him, "so now we have good water."

God continued blessing abundantly as Joe and Melody joined their efforts to the work that Sebastian, Ada, and Ray were doing. Soon fifty people were attending church each Sabbath, and the little building wasn't large enough. The Bible workers decided to build a new, larger, beautiful church. By the time the new church was completed, God had blessed them with eighteen baptized members, and an additional seventy to eighty individuals were attending Sabbath School and church each week! This is truly a "mission miracle"! God is pleased to work miracles on human hearts in response to the prayers and dedicated work of His volunteers.

Boys and girls enjoy the Sabbath School program at Kopinang.

The Battle to Make Time for God

God had plans to open the door to Guyana's big neighbor to the west—Venezuela—by beginning a medical aviation program in that country.

The seeds were sown when David was invited to participate in the dedication of a beautiful new church in Venezuela. The Amerindians had spent eight years building the church out of stone. During the dedication, the Amerindians asked Pastor Escobar, the Venezuelan director of ADRA, if he would start a medical aviation program for their region like the one in Guyana.

Pastor Escobar turned to David who was standing nearby. "Would you be willing to start such a program here?" he asked.

"I will certainly pray about it," David promised, remembering Paul's admonition to "make the most of every opportunity" (Colossians 4:5, NIV). "If it is God's will, I know He will open a way."

Several weeks later David decided to make a trip to Venezuela to see about the possibility of starting a medical aviation program. As he traveled to Caracas by land, David stopped to spend the night in the city of Puerto Ordaz. At the hotel, he was washing his dirty clothes when suddenly he received a strong impression that he must go immediately to the airport. "OK, God," he said aloud as he dried his hands, "I'll go if You want me to." And he called a taxi, wondering what surprise the Lord had for him at the airport.

The driver let him off at the first hangar, where four persons were waxing a gorgeous, four-seat Cessna Skyhawk 172. The chief mechanic and owner explained that Moody Bible Aviation had been flying this plane to Brazil for mission work when an engine failure had forced an emergency landing. The pilot guided the aircraft to a safe landing but not without bending the right landing gear. After settling with the insurance company, Moody Bible Aviation had decided to sell the damaged plane to him. He was a local air taxi operator, and he seemed very friendly.

David told him, "The Venezuela Union of Seventh-day Adventists has plans to begin a medical aviation service among the Amerindians of the Gran Sabana, near the border with Guyana and Brazil."

The owner of the plane looked at David and said, "Just today I finished the paperwork to register this plane in Venezuela for noncommercial use. In about three to six months I intend to sell it. Would you like to buy it?"

Wow! Talk about timing! David thought. *God has done it again!*

The next morning David returned to the airport with a substantial deposit from funds he'd been holding for the Venezuela project. He willingly went forward in faith, knowing he had a few months to pray that God would provide the balance of thirty thousand dollars.

Later, when he received notice that the owner had finished with his use of the plane and was ready to complete the sale, David called his dad, Richard Gates, in Illinois. "Have any funds come in to finish paying for the plane?" David asked.

"No," admitted his father. But he agreed to do as he had done for the mission planes in Guyana. Richard contacted a local bank and arranged for a ninety-day loan, using his bulldozer and tractor for collateral.

With the title in hand to the Cessna, David finished his medical and written examinations to obtain a pilot's license in Venezuela. By God's gracious mercies, the Venezuela Adventist Medical Aviation Service would soon take to the air.

But where would the thirty thousand dollars come from to pay off the loan?

It was at this time that David flew to Walla Walla, Washington, for a speaking appointment. That morning in Walla Walla, during his morning devotions, David seemed to hear God say, *You have done your part; the rest is My part!* A wonderful joy and peace filled David's heart all day. That afternoon, his father called to tell him that during the last two days, twenty-eight thousand dollars in donations had arrived for the plane. Normal monthly cash flow would be able to take care of the remaining two thousand dollars! Another mission miracle!

God had provided a plane, but it was worthless sitting on the ground in Venezuela with no pilot. David and Becky began to pray that God would provide a pilot. They knew it would not be easy to find someone with all the necessary qualifications. In their prayers, they gave God a tall order—a husband and wife team who was open to understanding other cultures and who was willing to live in contentment in circumstances that would be considered poverty in the United States. A couple who was compassionate, adaptable, capable, and willing to take risks for God. A pilot who was experienced and able to land and take off safely on short runways in difficult terrain. And on top of all that, it would be nice if one or both of them had nursing skills! It was a huge request; yet, David and Becky knew that God loves to do the impossible. They continued pressing their prayers to the heavenly throne daily.

The days passed, however, and they seemed no closer to finding the needed husband and wife team they needed to get the Venezuelan medical aviation service off the ground—literally. "I know God often answers prayer at the last minute," Becky said. "Let's not give up." And they didn't. Instead, they determined to maintain their faith and depend completely on the Lord.

Over a period of time, David had actually developed a list of twelve practical methods for doing just that—trusting God completely and depending on Him for all their needs. He kept the list in his Bible. Together, David and Becky decided this would be a good time to review that list. They had put these principles into practice many times before and had experienced God's blessings as a result. The list represented David and Becky's philosophy of mission service and provided a blueprint for their activities day by day. Here are the principles they reviewed in this situation:

1. If you feel unsure about a course of action or a decision, regular Bible study and prayer can confirm God's Word or the counsel

of the Spirit of Prophecy. (See Psalm 119:105; Proverbs 3:5, 6; James 1:5, 6.)

2. Ask God to make you willing to surrender all. Be willing to sever strong attachments to material belongings or any impure thing. When impressed to let go of something, obey joyfully. (See Matthew 26:39; Philippians 2:13; Romans 12:1, 2.)

3. Use prudent, sound judgment by following advice from mature Christians. Be sure the advice is in harmony with God's Word. (See Proverbs 4:10–13; 11:14; Isaiah 8:20.)

4. Avoid rushing recklessly into danger but throw yourself on God's promises and move ahead, even if doing the right thing seems risky. (See Matthew 4:6, 7; Romans 4:20–22; 2 Peter 1:4.)

5. If God gives opportunities to reach out in faith, don't hesitate. Listen to the Holy Spirit and act. Success requires action. (See Matthew 4:18–22; James 1:22; 2 Corinthians 9:6–8.)

6. Recognize that opportunities don't last forever. Prompt and decisive action at the golden moment will gain glorious triumphs. (See Galatians 6:9, 10; Ephesians 5:15, 16; Colossians 4:5.)

7. When obeying God's direct orders from His Word, move forward with confidence. When God says it is time to move forward, obstacles mysteriously disappear. (See Joshua 1:9; 3:14–17; Matthew 21:21, 22; Romans 8:31, 37.)

8. If you are already doing what God has commanded, you can count on His continuing guidance. If you've taken advantage of the opportunities He's given you, He'll provide for your financial needs. (See Matthew 6:33; Romans 8:32; 2 Corinthians 9:10, 11.)

9. The Christian life is all about balance. Do everything you can do with your unused resources. Remember, you don't really have any lack until you have nothing left. (See Matthew 6:19–21; 25:15–30.)

10. God loves to wait until the very last moment to provide for our needs. When you have placed all you have on the altar and nothing

is left, you'll experience maximum dependence and joy. (See Luke 10:1–4; 22:35; John 6:27.)

11. Develop a sense of urgency. The time in which we may work freely is short. What we don't give now will be of little use in the near future. (See Matthew 24:33; John 9:4; Romans 13:11.)

12. Put your assets where your mouth is and join those who are getting ready to meet Christ. Everything we own actually belongs to God. So, act now or get out of the way so others can. (1 Chronicles 29:14, 16; Haggai 2:8; Matthew 19:21.)

Of course, like everyone, David and Becky often had their own agendas and schedules. And they didn't always find it easy to keep these twelve principles in mind or to follow them faithfully. Sometimes they were tempted to overlook God's opportunities because of their own concerns. As they finished looking at the list once more, David recalled just such an occasion.

"I was flying from Miami to San Juan, Puerto Rico," David remembered. "As I was filing my flight plan, Manuel, an airport security official, approached me saying, 'You prayed for me when I had deep troubles. God gave me peace and cleared my guilt. Now I have many questions about God. Could you spend time with me and help answer some of my questions?'

"I'm ashamed to admit it, but my initial reaction was that I didn't have time to talk to Manuel. I wanted to keep on schedule and have a quick turnaround on this flight. Just then the fuel truck pulled up. So, as I was taking care of the fueling process, I said reluctantly, 'Well, Manuel, what is your first question?' And he replied immediately. It was an intelligent question about the Bible. And after that question, he had many more. He kept asking good questions. And all the while my conscience was pricking me. God seemed to be saying, 'Are you so busy being a missionary that you have no time for a Bible study with the honest seeker for truth?'

"One hundred five gallons later, the fuel man handed me the bill for two hundred ninety-four dollars. Manuel waved him away, saying to me, 'Come to my office. I'm paying this bill!'

"I yielded to God's strong impressions and postponed my flight until 11:00 P.M. Manuel and I spent the next five hours in his office poring over our Bibles. I noticed that he had already underlined in his Bible most of the verses we turned to as we talked about his questions. My heart thrilled as he gladly accepted one truth after another. Hours later, as I climbed into the plane, he announced, 'I'm going to honor God and keep the Bible Sabbath. Pray that I'll find the best way to tell my boss.'

"As I pushed both throttles and lifted the plane up into the dark, diamond-studded sky, I confessed, 'God, forgive me for almost missing that grand opportunity to share the gospel story.' "

In our hurried lives, Satan continually tempts us to miss those golden moments, but with each victory we become stronger to resist him. We need to pray King David's prayer,

> Be still, and know that I am God;
> I will be exalted among the nations,
> I will be exalted in the earth! (Psalm 46:10).

Quiet moments with God are so special that we cannot start the day successfully without them. As we read His Word and pray, we will feel Him directing us and assuring us that He is there to handle whatever may come to us during that day.

And in this confidence and assurance, David and Becky continued to press their petitions for a pilot for Venezuela—and to wait.

CHAPTER 4

Unexpected Challenges

Guyana Adventist Medical Aviation Services (GAMAS) urged David to make a special trip to Bolivia to look at an airplane that was for sale and that could be used in mission work in Bolivia. He went, and after finishing his business there, David attended an evangelistic meeting in the city of Santa Cruz. He was especially blessed by the special music provided by two women. One, who was blind, skillfully played the guitar, accompanying the beautiful voice of a younger woman.

"Who are they?" David asked someone nearby.

Jenny and Heidi use their many talents in ministry for prisoners in Bolivia.

"Two cousins, Heidi and Jenny," was the reply. "They are new converts who work as volunteers in the women's prison ministry."

As he was leaving, David stopped to thank the ladies for their music. When he introduced himself, both women began to jump up and down, praising God. "We've heard of your volunteer work," they told him. "We've been praying and fasting that you would come here soon."

Both of these women were from the upper class and had once been quite prosperous. Now they owned no warm clothing to protect themselves against Bolivia's cold southern winds. They walked to prisoners' homes to deliver donated clothes and food. Preparing legal documents on an old typewriter, they had managed to free thirty-five women who had spent more than eighteen months in prison without being charged.

During the next few days, David met many of the thirty-five former prisoners who had been released through the efforts of Heidi and Jenny. Many of these have been baptized, and others are attending the Adventist church. With extra donated funds, David purchased a warm jacket and a blanket each for both Heidi and Jenny, plus a computer to expedite their legal paperwork. Before he left, they all knelt in prayer asking God to provide a dependable four-wheel-drive vehicle so they could navigate the mud and terrible roads to visit the outlying homes of prisoners. Funds came in later so that David was able to purchase such a vehicle for Heidi and Jenny.

In an e-mail to David in early 2002 the two ladies stated, "We've been praying that God would provide for the expanding needs of our women's prison ministry in Santa Cruz. He has helped us to prepare more than a hundred women for baptism. With the computer we have prepared and executed legal proceedings to get more than ninety uncharged female prisoners released to go back to their families and children."

A few days later God impressed David during his private worship time to send Heidi and Jenny a monthly stipend, accompanied with the note, "What joy it is to be entrusted by God with funds so that none of God's workers will suffer for lack of basic needs. My plan is to do everything in my

David Gates stands with Jenny (left) and Heidi (right).

power to provide sufficient funds for God's proven workers to carry out the mission God has laid on their shoulders."

In Bolivia, children of prisoners may stay in the prison yard; they sleep on the ground near the prison wall. At least fifty children were living with their mothers in the women's prison, within the confines of prison walls and barbed wire. Heidi and Jenny were able to build a shelter for the children. Now they have begun a worship service in the prison every Sabbath. This began when Claudia, a dedicated Christian, received a five-year sentence for a crime she did not commit. Deciding to bloom

where she was planted, Claudia began a branch Sabbath School in the prison yard where the children lived. She also began giving Bible studies to several mothers. Jenny soon joined Claudia in the children's ministry program. As the group of children continues to grow, they wait and pray for God to send additional help.

Jenny and Heidi with a men's prison group to which they minister

About this time David had a speaking appointment in Tennessee. At the airport he met an old friend, Bob Norton.

"Tell me about yourself and your family," David said.

"Well, my wife and I have been thinking we'd like to close up our business and get into active mission work. My wife is a nurse and a native Venezuelan. And I've been working on getting some additional pilot's training."

David began to sense another "mission miracle." He turned to his friend and said, "Bob, we recently bought a four-seat Cessna Skyhawk one-seventy-two, a beautiful plane, but we have no pilot. Hundreds of Amerindians live in villages in that area with no medical help. I've been praying for a couple like you who understands other cultures and would be willing to volunteer. We can't give you a salary, but we can arrange for a place where you and your family can live. It isn't a place like you're used to here in North America, but we promise plenty of work and challenges. Are you interested?"

"I'll go talk with Neiba, and we'll pray for God's direction. I'll keep in contact," Bob promised. After talking it over and praying about it, Bob and Neiba sold two homes, their business, and almost all their other possessions in order to seize the opportunity to use their talents for God.

David purchased this plane, a beautiful Cessna Skyhawk 172, for use in Venezuela. Then he needed to find a pilot!

In June 2002, they landed in Caracas, Venezuela. Immediately, Bob ran into difficulties trying to process the proper paperwork to take a check ride and be qualified for a Venezuelan pilot's license. His introduction to Venezuela was made up of delays, long lines, frustration, wasted days, and unnecessary waiting. Finally, due to a combination of prayer, persistence, and miracles, Bob met the flight examiner at the airport, rented the use of an airplane for the test flight, and went over to inspect the plane. "The tires are threadbare, and the brakes are almost gone," he told the examiner, "but the rest of the plane seems good, and at least the fuel tanks aren't leaking. I couldn't find any maps, so we'll just have to keep track of where we fly. I'm ready to go."

The examiner climbed into the seat beside Bob. The flight went well. Bob made a nice, soft landing, and the examiner filled in the papers. Bob could feel God's presence during the check flight. The next step was to have the examiner's paperwork verified so Bob could receive his license. Early next morning he waited in line only to be told, "Come back in three days." Finally after much discussion, accompanied on Bob's part by silent prayer, the officials agreed he could return the next day. The next day the man who needed to sign the papers was at the office, but the government had declared a strike and no work was being handled. The following day was a Friday, and Bob knew that if he couldn't get his papers signed on Friday, he and Neiba would be stuck at the hotel for the weekend. He waited until six o'clock Friday evening. Still the official refused to sign, even though he knew how long Bob had been waiting. On Monday, Bob was back early. Fifteen minutes later, he had his Venezuelan pilot's license in hand.

The next priority was to get a taxi to the airport in order to catch a plane

Bob and Neiba Norton have dedicated their lives to mission service in Venezuela. Neiba is a nurse, and Bob is a pilot.

that would be leaving in two and a half hours. They arrived at the airport just in time to check in. It was a fifty-minute flight to the commercial airport nearest the college. But "near" was a relative term. To get from the airport to the college required a nine-hour bus trip. Bob and Neiba finally arrived at the campus of Colegio Gran Sabana, where they would make their home.

In February 2002, church administrators in the Venezuela-Antilles Union Mission invited David and Becky to come to their field and start the new medical aviation program and also to serve as a volunteer communications director and assistant ADRA director. What should they do? Should they leave Guyana? After much prayer, they left their home in Kaikan, Guyana, believing that God had called them to Venezuela— and trusting that He would continue to direct the consecrated team of volunteer missionaries they would leave behind.

David and Becky moved to Colegio Gran Sabana in Santa Elena, Venezuela. When they arrived, there was no available housing. So, David, Becky, and their two boys stayed temporarily in two rooms in the home of the boys' dean. When the Norton family arrived in June, the dean suggested, "We have one room left in our apartment. There's no other place on campus. Bob and Neiba, you may share the apartment with us and use the kitchen. So, three families made do. Bob and Neiba lived in that one room for seven months. Their son Josiah moved in with the Gates' boys.

One evening David received a call from Jenny in Bolivia. "David, remember you asked us to find out about broadcasting requirements here and to be on the lookout for any stations that might be for sale?" Her voice bubbled with excitement. "Well, even though Heidi is blind, she decided she would do what she could to find a station. So she called the tele-

David and Becky Gates with their extended family at their home in St. Elena, Venezuela

phone operator and asked for the number for each of the TV stations in town. Then she called the stations one by one and asked if the station was for sale. Most were very surprised by her question and emphatically said, 'No, of course not!' When she called Channel thirteen, she was told, 'No, but we do have a network for sale.' "

"A network!" exclaimed David. A network had not even entered his mind.

"Yes," Jenny continued. "The owners have two networks. They are involved in the national presidential campaign; so, they have decided to sell one network to fund the campaign."

"How much does this network cost?" asked David.

"Only a million dollars."

"A million dollars!" David almost fainted. "Jenny," he stammered, "you know we don't have that kind of money! Even if we closed down all our schools and aviation programs, it would still take several years to accumulate that much money."

"But David," Jenny argued, "don't you always preach that opportunities come from the Lord and that He guarantees the funds for their advancement? Just imagine how many multiple millions of people in Bolivia could hear the gospel if we bought the network. Could it be that God has bigger plans, a dream come true?"

"You're right, Jenny. I've seen God's hand at work too many times to doubt His ability and willingness to provide. Let's pray about it, and I'll consult the board of Gospel Ministries International at our next annual meeting."

Jenny and Heidi stand in the courtyard of the prison where they minister to those who are incarcerated.

For the board meeting, David prepared a financial statement that showed God had richly rewarded an aggressive expansion program by nearly doubling the funding every year for the last three years. When he shared this latest project—a one million dol-

lar television network—with his father, David expected a negative recommendation. His father was always conservative on spending. To his surprise, he heard his father say, "I'm convinced that Jesus' return is imminent. We shouldn't reject any opportunity simply because of the cost."

Later, the Gospel Ministries International board recommended moving forward with the proposed network purchase, knowing full well that the organization had absolutely no funds available for this project. Surely the Holy Spirit took things into His own hands and influenced the board to go forward in faith.

Can God supply more than one million dollars? Gospel Ministries International believes that He can. It believes in mission miracles.

Only a Million and a Half Dollars!

A few weeks later David and his father flew to Bolivia. Bob Norton accompanied them in order to get more experience flying.

First, they met the television network manager who explained, "Our company, Red Uno ["Network One"], has decided to sell our UHF network, Red Magica ["Magic Network"]. We designed this network for children's programming. It covers six of Bolivia's largest cities. For only a million and a half dollars, you would be getting a very good deal."

In Latin America large business transactions take place only between persons who establish a friendly relationship and who are of similar socioeconomic status. The manager arranged a meal in a fancy restaurant. This would allow the network owners and prospective buyers to meet each other. After some casual conversation, the television vice president asked David, Heidi, and Jenny to define their vision for the network. He seemed pleased at their focus on improving the physical, intellectual, and moral values of the viewers. Before their conversion, both ladies had been wealthy and raised in the top social strata of Bolivia. Educated with the elite, they had traveled with the Who's Who of the country.

In the eyes of the television executive, the match was perfect. He felt comfortable that the prospective buyers were suitable people. "We'll proceed with negotiations tomorrow morning," he told them.

The next morning, realizing their own smallness and inability, they knelt in a circle at Heidi and Jenny's house. "We confess our total dependence on You, God, for the outcome of these discussions," they prayed. "We ask for wisdom from on high to negotiate the purchase of this network which would bring the light of Your glory to millions in Bolivia. Our eyes are on You."

Later that morning, David, his father, Jenny, their lawyer, and their technical advisor entered the large boardroom. As the network manager led David to his seat, he whispered in his ear, "The president of the company has a reputation as a hard negotiator. Don't be surprised if he won't budge." He mentioned that the Catholic Church had also made an offer to purchase the network. David sat next to the president and owner of the network, a man so wealthy he could almost be considered the owner of the country.

As the discussion began, the president said, "Another organization wants this network; however, they have offered us only one million dollars. We are asking one and a half million dollars."

"One and a half million dollars!" exclaimed David, his head reeling. "I was told the price was only one million dollars!"

"You must have been misinformed," the manager replied. "We have been asking one and a half million dollars all along." He quickly produced some documents to prove his point.

David's knees began to shake as he prayed, *Lord, what should I do?* Quickly, the Bible story of the five loaves and two fish flashed into his mind. *If God can feed five thousand people,* David thought, *He could also have fed twenty thousand.* Then his father's quiet voice asked, "What's the difference, David—one million dollars or one and a half million dollars? You don't have either amount, but God does!"

The Holy Spirit convicted David that his father was right. Hadn't God said that all the silver and the gold were His (see Haggai 2:8) as well as the cattle on a thousand hills (see Psalm 50:10)? Wasn't it God Himself who said, " 'Open your mouth wide, / and I will fill it' " (Psalm 81:10)? David knew that God is pleased when we make the very highest demands upon Him, especially if it involves carrying forward His commission to go into all the world and preach the gospel. As these promises came to his mind, David felt God's peace and joy flooding his soul.

"We also want the network," David replied, "and we are willing to pay the one and a half million dollars you are asking."

"You are?" asked the owner. He seemed surprised that David didn't try to negotiate a lower price.

But David wasn't finished. "If we buy the network, we will need a place to work. So, we would kindly ask you to include in the deal the property you just purchased across the street that contains offices and a warehouse. We could remodel these into a studio. Second, we ask for visibility on your larger VHF network. We would like four thirty-second spots on prime time each day."

The gate at the entrance to the ADVenir property and offices in Bolivia

Now the owner really did look surprised. "But we just purchased that property so we could expand our station," he declared.

"I accepted your asking price," David replied firmly. "Now I ask you to accept my requests."

The owner turned to the man sitting next to him and whispered, "This 'gringo' sure is a hard negotiator." After some discussion, the owner stated, "We are willing to sell you the network. The final purchase price of one and a half million dollars will include the licenses and equipment for six TV stations, one year free use of our towers and stations to house the transmitters, the beautiful three-hundred-thousand-dollar property, and four prime-time spots each day for twenty-four months, worth seven hundred and thirty thousand dollars."

Can there be any doubt that God controlled these negotiations?

The formal ceremony for signing the contracts took place at the network owner's sixteen-acre estate on January 31, 2002. The ceremony was filmed by the network's news team, and a two-hour banquet followed. During the meal, the network owner, who was also running for public office in Bolivia, kept asking questions about the Bible. He asked for

The formal signing of the contract selling the network to Gospel Ministries International took place on January 31, 2002, following a series of negotiations.

advice on how he could best run his campaign and shape a government that would merit God's approval. Surely God arranged this opportunity to share His truth one-on-one with this person.

The big question remained, however: How would Gospel Ministries International pay for the network? David and the godly persons on the executive committee of GMI took God's promises in the Bible and the Spirit of Prophecy seriously. They believed that God is more than able and willing to provide for His work if His children move forward in obedience when He opens the door. Convinced that the earth is in its final moments of human history, they are convinced that there is no project of any cost that God will not fund if it is carried out in His way and at His command. The success of God's work cannot fail—except by our own willful disobedience and selfishness.

They put their trust in God's promise: "When the Lord gives a work to be done, let not men stop to inquire into the reasonableness of the command or the probable result of their efforts to obey. The supply in their hands may seem to fall short of the need to be filled; but in the hands of the Lord it will prove more than sufficient" (Ellen G. White, *Prophets and Kings*, p. 243).

The agreed-upon payment schedule was an immediate down payment of $100,000 with the balance of $1.4 million to be paid in two months. David's father arranged a bank loan for the $100,000 using the family farm as collateral, with the mission plane, a twin-engine Comanche, as additional security. As the two-month deadline for the final payment drew nearer, God's voice spoke to the GMI board members clearly in words from *Gospel Workers*, page 262: "Go forward. Let us obey the command, even though our sight cannot penetrate the darkness. The obstacles that hinder our progress will never disappear before a halting, doubting spirit. Those who defer obedience till every uncertainty disappears, and there remains no risk of failure or defeat, will never obey. Faith looks beyond the difficulties, and lays hold of the unseen, even Omnipotence, therefore it cannot be baffled."

Then came a phone call from Chip Doss of Edgemont Video. "David, I know it's about time for you to head south to Bolivia. What about your television studio? Do you need any equipment?"

"That is one of my concerns," David admitted. "I would really hate to fly the plane to Bolivia without taking along any essential equipment. But I haven't received any funds to purchase anything significant yet."

"Don't worry. We have enough professional studio equipment here at Edgemont Video to set you up with a skeleton studio. Come to Arkansas, and we'll make sure you have a plane full to take down," Chip encouraged.

A week later, David's heart rejoiced as Howard, Chip, and Jim Doss filled his van with studio equipment. Their willingness to give freely was evidence that God would provide for all future needs. David was more convinced than ever that God would never fail him as long as he continued to trust Him.

For the second time in 2002 the white-and-blue-striped Twin Comanche climbed out from Illinois on its thirty-two-hour flight to Bolivia via Miami, Puerto Rico, Venezuela, and Brazil. To date, the total resources for this television network were a one-hundred-thousand-dollar debt and about ten thousand in a bank account. But most importantly, David had a signed note from his heavenly Guarantor stating, " 'And whatever you ask in My name, that I will do, that the Father may be glorified in the Son' " (John 14:13).

Two evenings later, Becky and the boys had to watch David fly over their home in southern Venezuela as he headed south to Brazil; the schedule did not allow for an overnight stop. His sweet wife cheered him up on the HF radio, however, as he passed overhead. "I know you're flying to Bolivia without money to finish paying for the network," she said, "but this morning, during my devotions, I read Isaiah 55, and God encouraged me. I believe it's His promise to you. Won't you read it right now?"

So David pulled out his Bible and read,

"Ho! Everyone who thirsts,
Come to the waters;
And you who have no money,
Come, buy and eat.
Yes, come, buy wine and milk
Without money and without price. . . .
. . . I will make an everlasting covenant with you—
The sure mercies of David.
Indeed I have given him as a witness to the people. . . . "
". . . My word . . .
. . . shall not return to Me void,
But it shall accomplish what I please,
And it shall prosper in the thing for which I sent it"
(Isaiah 55:1, 3, 4, 11).

God's promises cheered his heart, just as they had encouraged Becky's heart earlier in the day.

During the entire trip David kept up hourly contacts with his dad on the HF radio. Just minutes after he crossed the border into Bolivia, he received an excited call from his dad that a check for one hundred thousand dollars had been delivered to the GMI post office box. The funds had come from an insurance settlement from the accidental death of a donor's wife. David's eyes filled with tears as he realized that sacrifice seems to be the common denominator among God's faithful people.

Arriving in Santa Cruz on Friday afternoon, David quickly unloaded the airplane and made his way to Heidi and Jenny's house for worship and supper. He spent Sabbath helping with an evangelistic campaign being conducted by the prison women's ministry. Sunday afternoon Jenny took him to the network offices and studio. She and other dedicated workers had spent weeks cleaning and refurbishing the studio and grounds. The property was now planted in new grass and nicely land-scaped. Holding up her blistered hands, she said simply, "God's network must reflect His character."

As the hour to meet with the network sellers drew near, David had one main concern. So he did what he always does in such situations; he prayed. "Lord, even when You do provide the funds, it seems it will be impossible for us to get on the air any sooner than a month from now. If we were to take ownership today of all six stations, we wouldn't be ready to go on the air. We don't want to have to use programming You can't approve. Please, Jesus, help us resolve this problem."

David and Jenny arrived at the network headquarters to find that the sellers were friendly but a bit uncomfortable. They were embarrassed, they admitted, because they hadn't yet completed all the legal paperwork needed to transfer ownership of the network. They apologized for the situation and asked, "Would you allow us another two or three weeks to finish the paperwork? Also, we've decided that we will pay the twelve thousand dollars in transfer taxes."

Delighted and thankful, David happily accepted their offer and breathed a prayer to his heavenly Guide not only for giving more time to set up the skeleton studio but for saving them money.

As the group continued preparing for the time they would go on the air, God was impressing dedicated individuals, both in Bolivia and outside the country, to volunteer their services to the network. Other offers of help poured in. Hispanic coordinators in North America made available or donated Spanish video material. Media centers in the Inter-American Division promised a constant flow of Spanish videos. In Colombia, the union signed a joint agreement to function as a full-time source for Spanish programs.

Meanwhile, GMI officially registered the network in Bolivia as RedADVenir (the He-is-coming Network). In English, it is called the ADVenir Spanish Televison Network.

As the end of April approached, both David and Becky felt God's presence. Peace and joy surrounded them as they again claimed the message in *Prophets and Kings*, page 243—"When the Lord gives a work to be done, let not men stop to inquire into the reasonableness of the command or the probable result of their efforts to obey. The supply in their hands may seem to fall short of the need to be filled; but in the hands of the Lord it will prove more than sufficient."

When David arrived again in Santa Cruz, he discovered that church members all over Bolivia were meeting in churches or homes to ask God to intervene in behalf of this wonderful opportunity to share the gospel. All over the country, songs of praise, prayers of thanksgiving, and Bible promises were ascending to heaven. This gave David much courage and joy.

On Monday, April 29, the local district pastor, Pastor Parada, Jenny, and David walked into the offices of the sellers once more. Unfortunately, ADVenir's lawyer was unable to come. All of the permits, titles, corporate papers, and financial fees were in order. But due to the lawyer's absence, the sellers agreed to postpone the ceremony until Tuesday, when both the attorneys for both sides could be present. Before he left, David handed personalized copies of *The Desire of Ages* and a vegetarian cookbook to each person on the sellers' team.

On Tuesday, as everyone was waiting to enter the boardroom, one of the men who had received a copy of *The Desire of Ages* shook David's hand warmly. "Thank you so much for that lovely book," he said gratefully. "My wife and I read one of the chapters yesterday. We have never read such a beautiful account of the life of Jesus. In fact, it brought tears to my wife's eyes."

When everyone was seated in the boardroom, the seller, who was running as a candidate for vice president of the country, announced that he was currently in the lead in that race. Evidently the people liked his policy of honesty and freedom from corruption. The seller agreed that only God could give his campaign wisdom and direction. He suggested that they all kneel down around the large table as David prayed for God's leading in the campaign.

During the meeting, David continually prayed silently, claiming God's promises for blessings. Three times he stepped out of the room into the bathroom to kneel before His Maker. Earlier in the day and throughout the meeting, he repeatedly tried to contact his father, but to no avail. When all the transfer process had been completed—except for the final payment—the seller suggested, "Keep calling your father; we can do what needs to be done tomorrow."

That night, David was able to contact his father, but no money had been received for the purchase of the network. "Press forward with confidence," his father advised. "God will reveal to you what you should say."

Waking up in the middle of the night, David wrestled with God for hours. At times, he considered admitting defeat and canceling the purchase. But at these times, God's peace left his heart. He began to doubt that God was really sufficient to make this purchase a reality. Then words he had read came to his mind: "Workers for Christ are never to think, much less to speak, of failure in their work" (Ellen G. White, *Christian Service*, p. 261). Instantly the thought came to him, *Call the sellers. Tell them you don't have the money. Their growing faith in God will enable them to understand.* With that thought came a wonderful peace.

The next morning David and Jenny met the company's vice president and treasurer alone. Jenny pointed to a framed promise from Joshua 1:9 that the owners had recently placed on the wall of the boardroom: " 'Be strong and of good courage; do not be afraid, nor be dismayed, for the LORD your God is with you wherever you go.' "

The administrators listened to David's explanation and asked, "How much more time do you need?"

David responded, "That's up to you. I can't define that when I know you really need the money."

With somber looks, they answered, "How about a month? We want to work with you because we know God will help you. Recently we have been offered two and a half million dollars for the network by another political party, but we share your same vision. We believe this should be God's station."

"Yes," agreed David, "this Spanish TV network project is not about money; it is about the precious souls that will be touched and brought to a knowledge of God and His soon-coming kingdom. God will complete the work He already has begun in the hearts of His trusting, obedient children."

During the next month, e-mails poured in from God's people who were praying worldwide. These messages came in English, French, German, Spanish, and Portuguese from at least twenty countries, including Norway, Romania, Spain, Australia, and Slovakia. Not only individuals but entire churches met to pray. One group met three times a day!

During this time, a close friend contacted David to express his interest. "I believe now is the time to place all on the altar," he told David. "It's time not only to commit ourselves but to put our resources at risk in God's work while we still control them. David, we're on your side; we're praying for God's work to succeed in this venture. Some influential persons don't believe that ministry resources should be placed at risk as you have done with this project in Bolivia. They are questioning your wisdom in pledging your twin-engine plane as security for the down payment of the network."

"Yes, I know," David answered. "But I believe God's work will never be finished if we are willing to use only cautious methods. As you know, a few short weeks after we signed the loan papers, God rewarded our faith by providing enough funds through a single donor to completely pay off the one-hundred-thousand-dollar loan for the down payment. The mission plane is no longer at risk.

"I believe that every resource God has placed in the hands of His people should be used *now* to leverage and advance God's work around the world," David continued. "I intend to use my influence, writing and preaching, to convince God's people that the time has come to stop running with footmen and begin contending with horses" (see Jeremiah 12:5).

His friend encouraged David, pointing out that God was giving this ministry special visibility at this time. In March 2002, the *Adult Sabbath School Bible Study Guide* featured the story of how an angel had delivered David from a gang assault in Lima. In May of that year, Pacific Press® published David's book *Mission Pilot*, with its thrilling account of miracles in Guyana. The *Adventist Review* had placed Heidi's and Jenny's miracles of faith on its front page in an article titled "Marked for Death."

"The real question is not about money," his friend concluded. "The question is, How can we fit into God's plan?"

"Hundreds are interceding in behalf of this Spanish network, and I thank God for that," David spoke with conviction. "All the angels of heaven are ready to cooperate with us. I truly believe that all the resources of heaven are ours when we are trying to reach lost souls."

But was God going to perform a mission miracle to finance the network? Those involved in this project believed He would. But meanwhile, they must do as Jesus told His disciples—"Watch and wait."

CHAPTER 6

Wrestling With God

On Sunday morning, June 2, 2002, while David prayed during his morning devotions, he received a very strong conviction that he must go to Bolivia immediately. He shared this with Becky, who confessed she had the same strong conviction. That same day, David talked with his mother who said, "I sense you must go immediately to Bolivia and resolve the payment issue."

So, he flew his twin Comanche to Miami, caught a commercial flight to Bolivia, and arrived Tuesday, June 4. He made an appointment with the sellers for 11:00 A.M. the next morning. Three special sessions of prayer and thanksgiving with the network staff gave David peace that God would instruct him what to do.

The next morning, he awoke early for an hour of prayer. Wrestling with God like Jacob, David boldly asked for answers from His Word. This dialogue with his heavenly Father seemed like a real conversation, with God speaking to him through Bible texts.

David: "Dear Father, months ago we felt impressed that You were directing us to purchase this network of TV stations for one and a half million dollars. Did we do what was right in Your eyes?"

God: " ' "Give them something to eat" ' [Matthew 14:16]. *When you moved forward to acquire a network, you were acting in obedience to Me.*"

David: "But Lord, if we moved forward in obeying You, why do we not now have funds to pay for the network?"

God: " ' "If you love Me, keep My commandments" ' [John 14:15]. *It is not your business to ask how or why—only to obey.*"

David: "OK, Lord. I understand. But today I'm faced with dealing with the sellers. You have given us the opportunity to 'feed' the millions and witness to the wealthy. But what do I tell the sellers? I need to know from You exactly what You want me to do."

God: " *'Be anxious for nothing, but in everything by prayer and supplication, with thanksgiving, let your requests be made known to God; and the peace of God, which surpasses all understanding, will guard your hearts and minds through Christ Jesus' "* (Philippians 4:6, 7).

David: "I think I understand. You are saying, 'Stop worrying.' But facing a payment of one point four million dollars or the cancellation of the purchase, I need to hear it clearly from You again."

God: *"How much clearer can it get? Just obey, and leave the worrying with Me. Remember John chapter fourteen, verse twenty-seven, ' "Peace I leave with you, My peace I give to you. . . . Let not your heart be troubled, neither let it be afraid." ' "*

David: "I've got it, Lord. I'm not to worry regardless of the size of the problem or challenge. I must depend totally on You. I must accept the gift of Your peace and totally rely on Your strength to solve the problem, even for one point four million dollars. Now comes the question I need answered. How much cash am I to offer? Another hundred thousand dollars that I could borrow as I did before? Please Lord, I need a *clear* answer—*how much?* "

God: " *'My God shall supply all your need* [in Spanish: "all the balance of your need"] *according to His riches in glory by Christ Jesus' "* (Philippians 4:19).

David: "Wait a minute, Lord! How much did You say?"

God: *"The balance of your needs."*

David: " I can't believe this, Lord. Could You mean exactly that? Or could You mean my minimum needs?"

God: *"I mean exactly what I said—the balance of your needs."*

David: "That would mean I should offer them a total of one point four million dollars this morning. Are You saying You will cover a check for one point four million dollars?"

God: " ' *"According to your faith let it be to you" '* [Matthew 9:29]. *My promise to you is that I will cover the check for the full amount if you write it for that. I will do according to your faith."*

David: "Your message is very clear. I praise and honor Your name. Thank You for allowing me the great privilege of being used by You to show the world how great You are and how much we miss by trying to finance everything by normal human methods. In perfect peace I will obey and will not worry. Thank You, precious God."

God: *"Thank you, My son, for trusting and moving forward in faith and giving Me such great joy. I impressed you from the first that this matter will not be solved through normal human means. I will do it Myself* '*that all the peoples of the earth may know the hand of the* LORD, *that it is mighty, that you may fear the* LORD *your God forever*" ' " (Joshua 4:24).

After a special season of prayer and praise with the television team, three individuals went with David to the meeting. When they arrived, the sellers seemed a bit tense and worried.

David began by saying, "First of all, I must let you know that I came prepared to pay the full balance of one point four million dollars."

Smiles registered on their faces as they leaned forward in their chairs to listen.

David continued, "For me this is a very sacred moment. May I share some spiritual details with you?"

They nodded.

"This is a project of faith," he went on. "God has never failed me, and He won't now. I didn't come to Bolivia prepared to give you a check for the full amount. But that changed this morning because of God's leading. May I share with you how God led me this morning?"

"Yes, of course," the vice president agreed enthusiastically. "We recognize that God has been blessing us in our political campaign since this partnership with you began. Please tell us what God did for you this morning."

As David guided them through his entire conversation with God, he asked Jenny to read each verse from the Bible. They listened with rapt attention, seeming to agree with each point. He concluded, "Now you know why I have written this check. At this moment, I do not have the funds to cover the check. My signature is not strong enough to cover a check for one point four million dollars. Since God is the Guarantor of this check, I wrote 'Philippians chapter four, verse nineteen' next to my signature to show who is really paying for the check. When this check is cleared by the bank, you will be God's witnesses and will be held accountable to God for sharing what you have seen Him do. Do you agree with that?"

With smiles on their faces, they said, "We know you are a man of God. When He speaks, you obey. We will accept God's guarantee for the payment and provide you with a receipt. We intend to support you and work with you in every way we can. Don't worry. We know God will stand behind this check."

Inwardly David marveled at the faith of these two Catholic men. He seemed to hear Jesus say, " 'I have not found such great faith, not even in Israel!' " (Matthew 8:10).

All five of them in the room knelt together and consecrated themselves and the check to God. After signing the official receipt and taking pictures, the sellers asked, "When can we deposit this check?"

"Any time. Right away if you want," David responded. "God's signature is always good." They laughed together, for they believed God was sufficient.

The $1.4 million check. David (right) stands with a representave of the network. The owners said, "We know God will stand behind this check."

David felt peace, for he knew that God is well pleased when His people "make the very highest demands upon Him, that they may glorify His name. They may expect large things if they have faith in His promises" (Ellen G. White, *The Desire of Ages*, p. 668).

CHAPTER 7

"What Happened to the Check?"

The birth of Red ADVenir, the Adventist Spanish Television Network, generated tremendous enthusiasm in the Hispanic membership worldwide. God's Spirit raised up volunteers, skilled professionals from eight countries, who volunteered to assist with the project. While the workers converted the larger building into the main studio, a smaller building was used as the office complex. Initial broadcast production focused on Bible study and children's programming.

In South America, two other denominational media centers signed agreements to focus programming over ADVenir on university youth and medical/educational topics. In North America, the Three Angels Broadcasting Network offered ADVenir access to any of 3ABN's programming materials. Two other media centers offered their support, and a second TV broadcasting station expressed interest in rebroadcasting ADVenir's signal.

As funds became available, construction of an uplink site accelerated to top priority. With satellite transponder rentals to cover the Americas and Spain becoming ever more attractive in

Initial broadcasts by ADVenir focused on children's programming and Bible study.

price, God was shouting at His people to accelerate. ADVenir staff felt that it was time to sprint to the finish line. That it was now or never!

Back in the United States, David met with his bank manager. He explained the situation and provided the bank with a photocopy of the check. After prayer together on their knees, the manager asked David, "What if the check arrives and we have insufficient funds to cover it?"

"No problem," David responded. "Treat it as you would any other check. If funds are there, pay it. If not, bounce it. My responsibility as a soldier in God's army is only to obey. The consequences of what happens belong to the Commanding Officer who issues the orders."

On June 12, David's cell phone rang midway across Wyoming as he and his family were driving to Washington state for a camp meeting appointment. When he answered the call, he heard his banker's voice on the other end. "David, the bank of Miami just called to advise us that the one point four million dollar check has arrived there. They called ahead to ask if we had sufficient funds to cover the check. We told them, 'No.' The check is now on its way here to us. We'll receive it tomorrow."

Fear wrenched David's stomach. The enemy whispered into his ear. *Now look what you've done. You've embarrassed yourself and God. The entire project will end up in bankruptcy, a total failure.*

As he drove, David, his wife, and their boys prayed. "Lord, we're afraid. You have never failed us before. We refuse to accept that You will fail now. Regardless of what happens, even if we don't understand, we cannot accept the failure of Your promises. Thank You for the opportunity to trust in You even though failure appears imminent."

Then Becky said, "Remember what Moses told the Israelites when they were standing helplessly before the Red Sea, surrounded by mountains, with Pharaoh's army closing in? He said, ' "Do not be afraid. Stand still, and see the salvation of the Lord" ' " (Exodus 14:13). Peace flooded the car and the heart of each trusting person in it.

Commenting on Moses' experience at the Red Sea, Ellen White wrote:

Often the Christian life is beset by dangers, and duty seems
hard to perform. The imagination pictures impending ruin before

and bondage or death behind. Yet the voice of God speaks clearly, "Go forward." We should obey this command, even though our eyes cannot penetrate the darkness, and we feel the cold waves about our feet. The obstacles that hinder our progress will never disappear before a halting, doubting spirit. Those who defer obedience till every shadow of uncertainty disappears and there remains no risk of failure or defeat, will never obey at all. Unbelief whispers, "Let us wait till the obstructions are removed, and we can see our way clearly;" but faith courageously urges an advance, hoping all things, believing all things (*Patriarchs and Prophets*, p. 290).

The next day, June 13, the cell phone rang again when they were driving through Washington state. The banker told David, "The check arrived late last night. We must respond to it today. The funds are still not here. What do you suggest?"

"Hold the check as long as you can today," David requested. "Then follow standard procedures. I'll call Bolivia and let the sellers know what is happening."

The great controversy raged in David's mind. Satan forced the thought upon him, *You need to fear. You acted alone and without direction. You dishonored God, and now you will reap the consequences!*

Again Becky opened her precious Bible. First she read the promise she'd read the day before and added, "Listen, David. God says to you, 'For God has not given us a spirit of fear, but of power and of love and of a sound mind' [2 Timothy 1:7]. ' "Peace I leave with you, My peace I give to you. . . . Let not your heart be troubled, neither let it be afraid" ' " (John 14:27).

The thought kept getting louder in David's mind—*"Do not be afraid! Do not be afraid! DO NOT BE AFRAID!"* Whatever direction his mind went, he still heard these words. The struggle became intense as he realized the choice: Fear versus God's promise of peace. Was God able to perform a miracle? David and his family chose to believe God's Word and accept His promise of peace. They began to sing as they drove, and the joy of victory rang through their songs.

A few minutes later, Becky turned on the radio, looking for a Christian station. Through the speakers came the voice of a preacher explaining how God has an ocean full of blessings waiting for us, but many times we take only a cupful. Tears sprang to Becky's eyes. "Oh, precious Father," she whispered, "I don't believe this is a coincidence. Thank You for Your encouragement. Forgive us for the many times we have only taken a cupful. Today we choose to take one point four million dollars, and I pray that this will result in bringing honor and glory to Your name." David and Becky felt added confirmation when at the end of the program they discovered that radio program was *The Voice of Prophecy* and that the preacher was Lonnie Melashenko.

When David called Jenny in Bolivia to let her know about the situation with the check, she replied cheerfully, "Yes, we've known since yesterday. The bank of Miami called the sellers to advise them about the insufficient funds. The sellers didn't seem disappointed or discouraged. They instructed their bankers not to return the check to Bolivia but to keep it in Miami. They assured the bank that the check was good and expressed confidence that very soon the funds would be on hand to cover it."

After the call, David turned to his wife and said, "I've come to believe that when God wants to take over a property, the owner really has very little to do with it. God's promises are equal to cash, and we must act on God's Word. God is calling us to detach ourselves totally from things and to depend on Him for all our needs. We must be willing to take the risk."

Following six weeks of intensive camp meeting appointments from Washington to Maine, David and his family headed back to the farm in Illinois to load the plane with medical and broadcasting equipment, as well as aviation and school supplies. David dreaded the lonely flight down to South America by himself, leaving his wife and boys behind. But he felt deep joy from the reports of how God was continuing to accelerate the work in Guyana, Venezuela, Colombia, and Bolivia.

In Bolivia, David met with the sellers once more. With no solution but armed with God's peace, he entered the boardroom. The sellers made it clear they needed the money to clear the network property title and pay other debts. Again, David offered to allow them to sell to another buyer.

"No," one of the owners interrupted him, "we aren't interested in selling the network to anyone else. The network belongs to you! In fact, our engineers asked us to have you take over operations as soon as possible. We believe your check in Miami will be paid. But we also beg you to help us in our desperate financial need. Would you please take over the operation of the network in the near future?"

Amazed at the humble demeanor of these rich men who weren't accustomed to begging, David asked, "Would September be an appropriate month for us to begin operations?" They nodded. "Regarding finances," David continued, "we have only prayer to turn to. God has consecrated children with sufficient resources. We are praying that He will tap them on the shoulder. If not, He still owns the world's gold and silver and has a thousand ways to provide for our needs. Would you care to pray with me now?"

"Will you pray for us?" they asked. "We really don't know how to pray." They knelt, and David prayed, "Gracious Lord, we confess our unworthiness. We plead with You to demonstrate Your power to provide for our urgent financial needs. Give us peace and take our worries." The owners had smiles on their faces and appeared relaxed as they arose.

As David walked to the studio, he made a mental inventory of the needs required to meet the September deadline to begin operation of the network. First, they must get the new digital equipment installed. Second, they must train personnel. Third, they must finish the large studio.

A little later, there was a knock at David's door. Marco, a young broadcast engineer in his thirties, smiled. "I've been asked by the network owners next door to come by and see if you need a hand with any technical matters."

"Please come in! Let's take a tour of our facilities and discuss the challenges of meeting our September deadline."

As they walked and talked, Marco made a list of the needs and placed them on a time line. Then he spoke. "A fully digital studio is something that none of our broadcast networks here in Bolivia have yet accomplished. You have very good equipment here, and this is a wonderful opportunity to get started on the right foot. Your crew also needs production training on this new equipment. May I use your phone?"

With only two phone calls, he lined up two expert technicians to train the new personnel at his expense. With another phone call, Marco called an Italian friend and whispered to David, "He has designed all the big studios in Bolivia. He's the best in the country, and he'll design your studio here."

The master control room at the ADVenir network. God blessed in a miraculous way in providing equipment and training to make the network possible.

Within days, workmen were crawling all over the building, pouring the floor and installing the ceiling, air conditioning, lighting structures, control rooms, and sound proofing.

"Besides getting the personnel and studio ready, what else can I help you with?"

Marco wanted to know.

"I've been wondering about the distribution of our signal to other cities," David replied. "I really would like to get our signal on satellite as soon as possible."

As usual, Marco had already done his homework. "I've contacted another TV network I work with that is using only nineteen hours a day of the twenty-four hours available on the NSS-806 satellite which covers both North and South America. For two thousand dollars a month they are willing to rent you the remaining five hours of satellite uplink time each day from one in the morning to six in the morning I suggest you accept their offer. This will give us time to iron out any wrinkles in our system. We will send them our signal by fiber optics, while at the same time we start building our own satellite uplink. Within a few months we should be ready to uplink twenty-four hours a day."

David marveled as he watched Marco direct the work. Surely God had sent this young man. By using the many small sacrificial donations that poured in to finish the studio and begin uplinking, God was effectively multiplying the loaves and fishes before his eyes.

Three weeks after the presidential election in Bolivia, no one knew which of the three top candidates had been elected. However, just before David left the country to return to the United States, he heard the news that Bolivia's future president had been selected. He was not the candidate belonging to the political party of the owner of the network. Immediately David recognized another call to prayer. "Please, dear Lord, according to Your will may the changes in the presidency and parliament continue to hold open the door of opportunity for Your work in the country of Bolivia."

God had worked so many miracles in this matter. What further miracles lay ahead?

CHAPTER 8

Volunteers Get Frustrated, Too

David continued to face the many challenges connected with the TV network in Santa Cruz, Bolivia. Bob, Neiba, and Josiah Norton also were experiencing a difficult time those first few weeks in Colegio Gran Sabana, Venezuela, in the summer of 2002. Bob spent much time working on the only available vehicle, a jeep, but it refused to run. To buy food meant that they had to go to Santa Elena, the nearest town. The teachers hadn't been paid in a month, because only fourteen of the more than seventy students at the school were able to pay their fees. The other students were working their way through school, but this didn't provide any money for teachers or food. After the Nortons learned that there wasn't enough food for the students, they decided not to eat in the cafeteria.

However, God always provided for their major needs. Bob found a ride into town. With personal funds, he bought food and some needed parts to fix at least some of the jeep's problems.

A month later, in July, Bob joined one of the teachers going to Puerto Ordaz, an eleven-hour drive from the school. The mission plane had been grounded at the airport there for about eight months because of delays in registering the plane properly. In Puerto Ordaz, Bob tried all day on his cell phone to call the ADRA director. At last he got through just an hour and a half before the director needed to board a plane for Caracas. He agreed to accompany Bob to see the Venezuela mission plane. At the airport, they talked with the plane's former owner, who gave them the papers needed to change the registration. But the registration papers had to be signed by personnel at the Venezuelan Union office in Caracas. The ADRA director offered to take the papers with him to Caracas. This saved Bob a bus trip to the capital—twenty hours each way! For Bob, it was just another evidence of God's perfect last-minute timing.

August was the month selected for a special dedication service in Santa Elena for the mission plane. Amerindian leaders from all the different

areas of the country would come to see the plane that would be visiting their areas to help them and their people. But the papers sent to the Union office in Caracas still remained unsigned. David, who had come to Venezuela for the dedication service, called the office, urging that the papers be signed and placed that night on the commercial flight to Puerto Ordaz. That way, they would arrive the night before the dedication service. Anxiously Bob and David waited for the flight to come in. But the papers weren't on that plane. Nor were they on the first plane the next morning. More phone calls. "They'll be on the twelve-ten plane," David was promised. Maybe,

Top: Bob and Neiba Norton (front row, center and right) stand in Santa Elena, Venezuela beside the new mission plane, dedicating it to God's work. Bottom: Many gathered for the dedication service; one elderly man laid his hand on the wing, thanking God for the help the plane would bring to his village.

just maybe, Bob would still be able to fly the plane in time to arrive during the afternoon program. But, again, there were no papers on the 12:10

plane. The airport agent said, "Maybe they'll be on the next plane." But would the plane arrive soon enough? Would they have to conduct the dedication service without the mission plane?

Bob was so upset he thought he would explode. He went outside and told God exactly how he felt. He stood looking at the plane, totally upset with many people, including church leaders who should have acted more responsibly. He dared not fly without proper registration. Now he was stranded without a way to get home! On top of everything else, today was his wedding anniversary. He vented his feelings to God's listening ear. "Lord God, I've done all I could. I've pleaded with You, but to no avail. You know if the mission plane doesn't arrive for the dedication service, a lot of eager people will be left in doubt and disappointment. It's Your problem, not mine!"

In the middle of his complaints, peace suddenly filled Bob's troubled heart. A Bible verse came bursting into his mind: " *'I have spoken it; I will also bring it to pass'* " (Isaiah 46:11).

He went back into the airport office. No papers could be found. "Please keep hunting. They have got to be somewhere. Perhaps they're coming on the next plane."

"Yes, another plane is due to land in ten minutes. Maybe, just maybe, they'll be on that one."

In faith, Bob thanked God for putting the papers on that plane. And, praise God, he had them in his hands at 1:40 P.M. Could he make it before the dedication program ended?

He ran to the plane, rechecked everything, prepared for the flight, and was off. He had clearance to land at the runway-in-progress at Santa Elena. Three hours later, he touched down on the first half of the runway (the rest wasn't yet finished). What joy! Everyone rushed to see their plane, the plane that would come and bring help to them. One old man came and laid his hand on the wing, saying, "Many times I've prayed that someday help would come to my village. Now I see it. Thank God." The many problems Bob had encountered vanished before that wrinkled, happy face.

Alas, the registration papers went back to the Union office with those who had come from Caracas to the dedication. Why? The name on the registration hadn't been changed yet! That was the reason the papers had gone to the Union office in the first place! A few days later Neiba went to the Union office in Caracas to try to get the papers completed. The officers suggested, "Go back home, and we'll complete them and send them to you."

But she replied, "No, thank you. I'll stay right here and wait for them." The officers weren't pleased, but they did complete the papers!

Although such experiences were frustrating, Bob and Neiba better understood each day why God so often developed their patience by saying, "Wait on the LORD" (Psalm 27:14). Getting fuel to fly the plane continued to be extremely difficult. When fuel was available, they had to wait in line for hours. On one occasion Bob repeatedly called the airport in Puerto Ordaz to see if he could purchase some fuel, but no one answered the phone. Finally, in desperation, he prayed, "God, I have just a little fuel in the plane's tanks, just enough to take needed medicine to a small village with a very short runway. After that, I'm grounded. Show me what to do."

Bob spoke with the driver of the school's truck. "Is there any way you could take me to Puerto Ordaz to get fuel for the plane?"

"Well," the driver replied, "the starter isn't working, and the truck needs other repairs, but if you are willing to take the chance, let's go for it. The school could use some more food. It will take nine to twelve hours each way!" They loaded the two large airplane tanks onto the truck and by 4:00 P.M. they started for Puerto Ordaz. With God's blessing, they arrived early the next morning and immediately went to the airport to see about purchasing some fuel.

"No, we can't sell you fuel, for we have very little left in our tanks," the technician shook his head.

"Is there anyone else I can talk to about getting fuel?" Bob wanted to know as he prayed silently for God to show him a way to get what he needed so badly. He had a letter with him from the mayor of Santa Elena; he hoped that might help.

"Maybe the commander of the national guard would give you an official permit."

After the commander read the mayor's letter, he nodded, "Yes, I'll sign the permit and apply my seal. Take this to the fuel office and fill your tanks."

"Thank You, Lord," Bob prayed as he drove the old truck to the pumping station. Just then six airport officials ran toward him, "Stop! Don't fill those tanks. We must see a letter from both the fire station and the police of your town stating that your truck is in good condition to haul fuel." Santa Elena didn't even have a fire station! The officials went back inside while Bob waited.

"Now what, God? You know that I can't save lives without fuel to fly."

When the officials didn't return, Bob felt impressed to return to the National Guard commander and tell him what had happened.

"Didn't I both sign and seal a permit to fill your tanks? Go fill them!" he told Bob.

"Thank you," Bob replied and left. After finally filling the plane's tanks and loading them on the truck, Bob had another prayer on his lips. "Lord, we've had to push this truck every time to get it started. We don't dare do that in front of these officials. Please let it start on its own this time." And it started!

Before leaving town, Bob had to buy food for the school. Just as they got on the road out of town, the linkage for the clutch broke. "We'll have to get it welded," the driver said. Eventually they were back on their way, but the load was so heavy they had to drive more slowly than usual. It took twelve hours to get home, where Bob found an urgent radio call waiting for him.

A boy with an arrow in his arm needed medical attention. His parents had walked eight hours to get to a radio to call for help. So, Bob was up at five o'clock the next morning to get the plane ready. On his return, the ambulance waited at the airport to take the boy to the hospital. Immediately, Bob flew back to the same village where he had picked up the injured boy—this time for a pregnant mother whose baby was about to be born and who wasn't doing well.

Back in Santa Elena yet again, Bob headed for the mayor's office to get a permit to haul fuel. "You really don't need it, but I'll write out an additional permit for you not only to purchase more fuel but to transport the fuel as needed. Now, I have a favor to ask of you. A mother and her newborn baby need to get to her village. We don't have money to feed her or a place for her to stay. They live in Apoipo, about a twenty minute flight."

"I'll be glad to take her home. Bring them to the plane." Soon he was in the air once more. A few minutes later, he landed on a very narrow strip with a bad crosswind. He stopped the plane and opened the door. But the woman shook her head, saying something in Apari—a local dialect. Bob realized, then, that her limited Spanish and his inability to speak Apari had caused a problem. He was at the wrong village! But after only ten more minutes of flying time, she smiled broadly, saying, "Home! Home!" as the plane landed in her village.

Thinking how wonderful it would be to get back to his own home and be able to rest, Bob was preparing to take off when a man came running toward the plane. "My brother fell off a horse," he said. "He is in lots of pain. Maybe he broke his collar bone. He can walk a little."

"Bring him to me, but hurry. It will be getting dark soon," Bob instructed. By the time they landed in Santa Elena, he barely had time to get someone to take this latest patient to the hospital and then fly to his home base at the school before night came.

But Neiba's welcome made Bob forget his hours of frustration trying to get gasoline and the long day of flying. Together they rejoiced to be joined in service for God. What did it matter that more than half the time there was no running water in the house? They still had a barrel of water outside to use until the power came on again.

When fuel of any kind seems impossible to get, when the government cannot seem to solve the fuel crisis, when the school's food supply is desperately low, when there is no gas to go to town to buy supplies, Bob and Neiba tell God, "This is Your work, not ours. Calls for help from the very sick keep coming, but the airplane's fuel tanks are empty. We have no way to move forward. We put all our needs—everything—in Your hands, God. We are powerless on our own, and we simply wait and watch for You to open doors."

And God works miracles to allow His work to continue. During those first three months of 2003, the fuel crisis continued, but God provided enough gas to keep the plane flying so that many are alive physically and have had the opportunity of hearing the good news of salvation. In January 2003, Bob flew a total of twenty-two hours of emergency flights, taking patients to the hospital who had no other way of getting there for urgently needed medical care. Add to that more than four hours of flying time spent taking doctors or nurses to provide health care in the villages. And another ten hours bringing food supplies and spiritual help as he flew pastors and lay workers to outlying villages.

In February, Bob flew over sixty hours. By March, the total for the first three months of the year rose to more than one hundred thirty-four hours in the air. Somehow, God miraculously provided fuel for all these flight hours during a fuel crisis in Venezuela that lasted for months.

Does God work miracles to keep airplanes flying? Ask Bob Norton.

CHAPTER 9

God Controls His Work

In the summer of 2001, God impressed a young couple, John and Sue Bartels, to volunteer themselves for God's service. After searching for God's direction for several months, they were finding nothing but closed doors. Then—through a series of divine providences and a friend who had heard David Gates sharing his great vision for reaching the world for Jesus via television—the Lord directed John and Sue to call David. When John spoke to David about working as a broadcast engineer, David replied, "I started praying for an engineer only two weeks ago!"

He explained to John the volunteer opportunities available. Would John and Sue be willing to sell their home, cars, and most of their belongings? Would they give up a well-paying, reliable engineering position in Washington state and step out in faith with their two small children, Steven and Sarah? After much prayer, both Sue and John decided to ask the Lord to take away John's job if He indeed wanted them to work for Him in broadcast engineering.

Just before Christmas, John was laid off from his job; God was prepar-

John and Sue Bartels with their children Sarah and Steven. Through a series of providences, God opened the way for the Bartels to work for Him in Grenada.

ing the Bartels to move to Grenada, a small island north of Venezuela in the West Indies. John and Sue moved forward in faith and put their house up for sale before the year ended. John became unemployed on March 1, and many tests of their faith followed. Packing, selling excess belongings, purchasing video equipment for the station, securing a twenty-foot shipping container, making arrangements for its shipment to Grenada, and researching details of broadcast engineering were only a few of the many tasks that consumed their every minute.

As the months rolled by, their savings neared rock-bottom. Would God sell their house in time? Would He provide for their needs? Then, in June, just when it was most needed, John discovered some paper-work indicating that a previous employer owed him money. When he called, the human resources representative told him, "That money should have been paid to you when you left employment two years ago." God had reserved just enough money to keep the Bartels going when it was needed most!

By the end of August 2002, their house still had not sold. Funds were dwindling, and so was their faith. John called David and told him of the completely impossible situation he and Sue faced.

"Why don't you go to Grenada and get the project started," David asked. *Did he hear me?* John wondered.

Then David explained that everyone who prepares to do God's work runs into roadblocks that the devil puts in their path to discourage them. But when we step out in faith, God overrules the devil, and the road-blocks disappear. Sue was convinced, but John was hesitant. Could he leave his wife and two small children alone to finish such a large task and so many seemingly impossible obstacles? After much prayer, he felt that God was leading him. John purchased airline tickets to Grenada and prepared to get the project there started.

Once in Grenada, John began renovating an old concrete building that had been a doctor's clinic. There were no kitchen, bedrooms, or complete bathroom. Nor were there any useable plumbing or electrical systems. But when completely renovated, this 1,350-square-foot build-ing would become a two-bedroom, one-bath apartment with a television station and a small studio. Six weeks of hard work in Grenada flew past. With the help of two hired workers, he tore down the old walls, installed new plumbing, and made preparations for a group of twenty-three volunteer missionaries from the Templeton Hills Christian School who would be arriving shortly to help with the project. When the group began working, it was amazing to see how much work they could accomplish in a week! John was thrilled. New walls were constructed; windows, plumbing and electrical conduit were installed; the project leaped forward.

Near the end of his initial time in Grenada, John learned that his prayers had been answered when Sue told him on the phone, "The house has sold, and God has moved every roadblock out of the way." John knelt and thanked God for His wonderful blessings.

However, back home in Washington state, John and Sue were once again faced with God-sized trials. The sale of their home became mired in red tape, and bills began to stack up. They had only two hundred dollars left. John was sick and stressed. Awake in the middle of the night, he was studying the Sabbath School lesson when the Lord directed his attention to the thought exercise at the bottom of the page for that particular lesson: "Write down all the reasons you have faith in Jesus."

John went to his computer and began listing reasons for his faith in Jesus. When he finished, he heard the question ringing in his mind, *"So, do you trust Me?"*

"Yes, Lord," John answered through his tears. "But I need something to hold on to!" He picked up his Bible, and it fell open to Matthew 10. As John read verses 5 through 10, he realized God was telling him to go work for Him in Grenada, trusting Him for absolutely everything.

Two weeks later, God overruled the problems surrounding the sale of their home, and the deal was completed. John, Sue, Steven, and Sarah said Goodbye to their families and began their journey to Grenada. They arrived on March 18, 2003, after spending a couple of months at 3ABN gaining hands-on experience in broadcast engineering. Their two-bedroom apartment at the television station still needed a lot of work, but with persistent effort by John and Sue, as well as God's continued blessings and the support of the Grenada Mission administration, they made significant progress on both the house and the broadcast studio. The studio would become the Caribbean Family Network (CFN). CFN's mission would be to meet the needs of English-speaking Caribbean people while seeking to protect the national and regional culture by featuring Caribbean people in its productions. CFN was to be unique as a Christian television network; its focus on children, health, education, spiritual music, and Christian programming gave it a family orientation. All of this was designed to draw viewers to Jesus Christ. John and Sue trusted God to work mission miracles in Grenada, and they pressed forward in faith.

In September 2002, about the same time that John and Sue were preparing to broadcast from Grenada, Red ADVenir, the Spanish Adventist television network in Santa Cruz, Bolivia, began nationwide broadcasting via satellite uplink. Initially, the station rented five hours of satellite uplink daily from a local TV network. Then ADVenir downlinked the five-hour signal and broadcast fifteen hours daily throughout Bolivia on its own network of UHF television stations. ADVenir covered six of the nation's major cities and one small town. By year's end, ADVenir's own uplink was expected to begin twenty-four hour operation, covering South and Central America, the Caribbean, and most of North America.

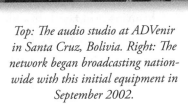

Top: The audio studio at ADVenir in Santa Cruz, Bolivia. Right: The network began broadcasting nationwide with this initial equipment in September 2002.

One day a man surprised David by asking, "What do you need for your broadcast work?" David knew that this man had earlier said that he never intended to use his money to finance a missionary.

"I'm praying for a hundred thousand dollars to buy a satellite uplink," David replied.

"I'll pay for half the cost, fifty thousand dollars," the man said, "if you can find another individual to match my donation." He paused and smiled at the incredulous look on David's face. "I know you prefer not to do fund-raising, but I suggest you put that aside for now and make a few phone calls to some of your friends."

David was caught completely off guard. He wondered what could have prompted this man to make such a generous offer for missionary work. "Thank you for your kind offer," he said. "Give me some time to pray about this. I'm sure God will provide someone to match your donation."

As soon as he was alone, David turned to the One he knew he could depend on. "Please, God, tell me if You expect me to break my commitment not to become involved in raising funds. Should I begin looking for a matching donor?" A clear response came to his mind—*"Finding resources for My work is My responsibility. Don't worry about this offer; I'll take care of it."*

Several days later, on a commercial flight from Puerto Rico, David was scanning through hundreds of new e-mails. A dollar figure in the subject line of an e-mail flashed across the screen and caught his attention. The message read, "I plan to send $50,000 for the ministry within the next two weeks. Where would you like me to send it?" In amazement David saw that this e-mail had been sent on the exact date that his acquaintance had made the unusual offer of a matching donation!

With a heart overflowing with gratitude to his Master, David thought of the promise in Nehemiah 2:20: " 'The God of heaven Himself will prosper us; therefore we His servants will arise and build.' " Aloud, he said, "Lord, I've given this work totally to You. Help me to follow Your directions and not what humans suggest. Thank You for making Yourself responsible for the needs of Your work."

Another mission miracle! God is more than able to keep His work moving forward.

A short time later David was in northern Bolivia near the Brazilian border. He took time to visit the church members of the Guayaramerin church. "Please let us take you to Yata village," they requested. "No Adventists live there, but the residents are very friendly and anxious to have an Adventist school near their town. We have explained our Christian philosophy to the village people and their leaders. Now they have offered to give us property for an industrial school."

David gladly joined them as they showed him the excellent plot of land the Yata villagers had made available to them. It consisted of 385 acres with a half mile of road frontage and a beautiful stream that wound along one side of the property for 1.7 miles. Two Bolivian families and a university student had already volunteered to live and work on the property.

David sipped a cool tamarind drink as he sat down with the villagers. "We greatly appreciate your generous gift." He smiled at his new friends. "With volunteer labor you can clear the land and build thatch-roofed classrooms and housing for staff. If everyone does his part, we can expect to begin classes with a full staff of volunteer missionaries. Since you have also offered to donate property in town for an Adventist church and parsonage, we can only dream of the impact an industrial school will have on church development and the blessings it will bring to this whole village."

The people nodded their approval, and one man spoke. "We believe in God. May we tell you how God spared the life of a lady right here a few months ago?"

"Please do!" David looked eagerly at the speaker.

"One day," the man said, "our quiet village of Yata was interrupted by loud cries. We all looked out our windows and doors to see a taxi speeding through town in a cloud of red dust. Before long we saw a man running his hands through his hair as tears ran down his face. 'My wife is dead!' he wailed. 'She just drowned.' He was making his way up the riverbank toward the only house with a telephone. 'My car ran off the ferry and fell into the water with my wife trapped in it,' he managed to blurt out. 'I got out, but my wife couldn't. People are struggling now to get her body out of the car. Please, may I call my children to let them know their mother has drowned?'

"Local village ladies covered their mouths with their hands and looked on in quiet grief, sharing this unknown man's agony. The man took the phone card a lady handed him. His hands trembled as he dialed the number. 'Son, it's your father,' he spoke into the telephone. Sobs interrupted him before he could speak again. 'Your mother . . . your mother drowned when our car fell off the ferry. I got out, but she's still trapped inside at the bottom of the river.'

"News travels rapidly in Yata village. Soon many curious adults and children poked their heads through the windows to get a glimpse of the wet stranger and hear his words. Others rushed to the river to watch people trying to pull the dead woman's body from the vehicle that was submerged upside down eighteen feet below the surface of the water.

"Everyone was watching the sad drama inside the house, so no one noticed a fat Indian *Acholita* [a woman from Peru] walk up behind the crowd. Though it is hot in the jungles of Bolivia, this woman was still wearing the many skirts that the women wear in the high Andean mountains. Her garments were at least five layers thick. Naturally this contributed to the size of her waist. Her thick black hair was formed into two large braids, tied at the bottom with a short length of black cord from which hung small flowers. Not wanting to miss a word of the poor husband's phone conversation, no one in the crowd wanted to give way to the *Acholita* as she tried to push herself through the mass of people—that is, until they noticed she was getting them all wet!

" 'Please, please, let me through. I must get through,' the disheveled lady kept saying as she pressed through the crowd. Finally she found the man she was looking for—the man on the phone! She pulled at him from behind, and he turned around and gasped at the sight of his 'drowned' wife. She threw her arms around him. Excitedly, she began to describe what had happened.

" 'A large bubble of air was trapped inside the car,' she said. 'It kept me alive as I struggled to get the door open. Finally, after about twenty minutes, I succeeded.'

"She had popped to the surface, pushed her way through the people, and began to hunt for her husband."

"Thank you." David smiled. "Thank you for sharing this miracle of God's love and grace right here in Yata village. I'm sure this is only the beginning of what God will do in this place for you."

CHAPTER 10

God's Work Will Succeed

David and a team of volunteers stood on the edge of the Andean highlands at an elevation of twelve thousand feet. With eager anticipation they looked over a great canyon where two million people live. The night lights of La Paz, Bolivia, lighted up the entire valley as far as the eye could see. All day long they'd worked setting up the equipment at the transmitter site. Now the question was, Would the ADVenir transmitter cover the entire city of La Paz? An hour after sundown, standing on the edge of the high plateau, they used their cell phone to call friends in each area of the city.

Each call produced an excited and happy voice, "Yes, the TV channel is on the air!" The city's largest cable network also carried the signal. Never before in history had the church in Bolivia had access to so many homes, rich and poor. Now two million people could view the good news of Jesus' love and soon return!

As they drove down to the city across cold, muddy, cobblestone streets, they noticed that the largest electronics store in La Paz had tuned its wall full of

Overlooking La Paz, the capital of Bolivia, home to some two million people. As ADVenir began broadcasting God's message throughout the city, miracles began to take place.

television sets to ADVenir. They saw people in several restaurants crowded around TV sets fascinated at what they were viewing.

In a new way, God's hand of mercy was reaching down to the people in La Paz. That night a desperate single mother decided that life was no longer worth living and was planning to kill her young daughter and then kill herself. Her daughter "happened" to tune in to ADVenir. Hearing the beautiful, peaceful music, the mother went to see what her daughter was watching. Was evangelist Alejandro Bullón speaking directly to her? As an invitation scrolled across the screen at the close of the program, she noted the address and rushed to the station.

She received Bible studies and began attending church each Sabbath. Today, her educated voice and clear, beautiful diction is part of video Scripture readings and other special spots on ADVenir. Another soul has come to Jesus! Another mission miracle!

Shortly after the network began broadcasting, the telephone rang, and an excited male voice exclaimed, "I stayed up all night to watch your broadcast, and I discovered something special about your late-night pro-

gramming. I find it has different, deeper thoughts and ideas than what you air in the daytime."

As Jenny listened, she thought, *So, someone has noticed that our satellite programming is more direct and digs deeper into the Scripture truths late at night.*

The person continued speaking rapidly, "I invited my church pastor and other members to come to my

The tape library at ADVenir. Late-night programming would dig deep into Scripture and present Bible truths.

house with their Bibles and watch. We closely followed Doug Batchelor's series [in Spanish translation] with our Bibles open. And then he taught about the seventh-day Sabbath."

Jenny's heart began to beat faster as she thought, *Perhaps I should have waited longer before I put that on the air.* She continued listening.

"No matter how hard we searched, we finally had to admit that the Bible does teach that the seventh day is the Sabbath. We belong to an Assemblies of God church that keeps Sunday. I thought you might be interested to know that our pastor and those members who gathered with me each night to watch your programs have now started keeping the seventh-day Sabbath."

This was the third time ADVenir had been contacted by Assemblies of God church members. The first two requested permission to retransmit the network's signal to community TV stations. All three contacts appeared to be totally unrelated. Truly the Spirit of God is working on humans who long to accept truth when they see the clearness of His Word.

Four major cities in Bolivia, plus many smaller areas, began transmitting ADVenir. After the network had been on the air only three weeks, the number of viewers had quadrupled. In Argentina, ADVenir was carried on seven cable networks throughout the country. Even a taxi driver from Brazil who spoke Portuguese and had been watching the five hours carried by satellite, requested, "Please hurry and begin transmitting twenty-four hours a day. I want to be able to watch it all day long!"

The receptionist at ADVenir greeted a caller warmly. The lady's voice sounded as if she had been crying, "I'm desperate for help. I realize I need Jesus' power in my life. Could someone from the studio please come and visit me?"

The receptionist transferred the call to Jenny. "I'll come this afternoon," Jenny promised the caller. "Please give me your street address."

Later that day Jenny knocked on the door of a large house in a plush neighborhood. A maid led her into the living room, and soon she heard footsteps.

"Thank you so much for coming," the lady said as she entered the room. "I keep my TV tuned to your station because your programs encourage me. I'm wrestling with a drinking habit that seriously affects my family."

After she shared her life story, she added, "Today the pastor on your TV program convinced me that God loves me and is willing to change me. I've decided to let Him control my life. What must I do now?"

Jenny shared the wonderful news of forgiveness and freedom in Christ with her new friend. The lady interrupted, "Tell me about this new network." Jenny explained how God had made it possible to get on the air. She shared how the sellers of the network had been patiently allowing ADVenir to continue broadcasting even though the group had not been able to finish paying for the station.

"I know Ivo, the owner," this lady said. "In fact, I grew up with him, and we're still close friends. We chat several times a week." She picked up the phone and dialed his number.

"Hello, Ivo. I'm calling about the ADVenir network. I just found out that you sold them the station. You can't imagine what a blessing these programs have been to me. Their broadcasts have changed my life. They're helping me overcome my problem with alcohol. Thank you for keeping them on the air."

But with all the evidence that God was directing this project, David still lay awake at night agonizing about the $1.4 million due in a short time. "Precious Lord," he prayed, "surely You haven't brought us this far to let everything fail!"

Becky, too, with fear gripping her heart, wrestled over the huge debt plus the continuing operating expenses, future satellite costs, the schools being operated in four countries, and the medical aviation program in three countries. All these operations needed assistance. "Dear Jesus," she added her prayers to her husband's, "we're so far out on the limb financially. Now I feel that the limb is about to be cut off. Please tell us what to do."

Instantly God responded to her plea, pointing her to the promise in Deuteronomy 33:27: " 'The eternal God is your refuge, / And underneath are the everlasting arms.' " She remembered the overwhelming evidence that God was in control. Her fear disappeared, and she rested in the joy that God could keep her singing His praises if she trusted completely in Him. She knew that God is able to solve the most drastic financial problems.

Before leaving Bolivia in late December, David wrote a grateful letter to the sellers of the network. "Thank you for your patience this past year.

I will no longer ask you for another extension. God continues to help us improve the well-being of the nation, blessing millions of viewers. The ratings show a shift of viewers to our network from commercial stations carrying violent programming.

"Although I have complete confidence that God is totally in control of the finances for His network, I will abide by your decision regarding the sale of the six television stations. Whatever your decision, it will not affect our ability to produce and uplink a full-time signal to the Hispanic world since the studio equipment and satellite uplink belong to us."

On December 30, 2002, the sellers called. "David, our board met last week and discussed your letter. First of all, we agree that you are accomplishing the goals we laid out in selling you the network. Second, we think you must get your satellite uplink going full time, and that might require a few months. The increased visibility and credibility will be a tremendous asset to you."

The voice paused as David listened for the verdict. "We decided not to demand the full amount at this time. However, as we mentioned to you before, we owe some heavy taxes which must be paid. David, we will be satisfied if you could give us only five hundred thousand dollars at this time. Could you do that?"

A lump crept into David's throat as he realized that even this smaller payment of a half million dollars depended solely on God's timing.

He replied, "I'm always amazed at your kindness and commitment to helping us remain on the air. Your request for half a million dollars is more than fair. Thank you so much." As he hung up the phone, David knew that what God decides to accomplish will succeed.

After talking with the sellers, David spent a few minutes reminding himself of all the evidence that God remained in control. His miracles were evident. He had always provided enough resources to cover the basic needs of each project. David felt blessed with an ever-expanding team of spiritually strong volunteers and donors who sacrificed to make growth possible.

The television viewing audience had grown from half a million to well over six million people in Bolivia alone. Nighttime satellite viewers reported watching ADVenir from ten countries. David knew that when the full-time satellite uplink facility was completed, the number would swell throughout the Americas and Europe. New broadcasting facilities were being built in Grenada, Bolivia, Venezuela, and Peru. However, to avoid non-Christian programming, David and his staff had chosen to honor God and terminate the partnership with the TV station in Guyana, thus avoiding conflicts.

Sufficient funds to cover the down payment for the TV network and to cover the purchase of the uplink facility had been donated exactly when needed. Surely the delay in paying the $1.4 million balance had not been accidental. "What important lessons can we learn from this?" David asked God. He remembered how God had given tremendous success so far. Surely, it would be a sin to doubt Him now. Success doesn't depend on the amount of resources at hand but on a willingness to trust God and move forward in obedience. David knew that God provides opportunities to give in order to bless the giver. The blessing is not in the amount given but in the attitude and sacrifice of the giver. The means and timing God chooses to provide for His work will frequently be unexpected and outside our normal way of thinking. He teaches us not to look to human methods. We must depend totally on the infinite resources of our Leader who claims that " 'the world is Mine, / and all its fullness' " (Psalm 50:12).

In early January, David, Becky, and their two boys flew to Venezuela. En route they stopped in Guyana. During board meetings at both Davis Indian Industrial College and Kimbia Mission Academy, the schools reported an overflow of students. The chief education officer of Guyana commented, "There are no schools in the entire country of Guyana like these Adventist schools."

Hardly had David touched foot back in Venezuela when the mission president called him aside. "A national television network has contacted one of our church members with an interesting proposition. He wants to see us right away."

Sensing that this was another divine appointment, they stopped for a season of prayer and Bible study. With a sense of peace they headed for the office of the network owner in Caracas. After some time getting acquainted, the owner stated, "When I was a child, my grandmother took me to the Adventist church every week. When I became aware that AD-Venir was on satellite four hours each night and would soon be on broadcasting twenty-four hours a day, I decided I would like to rebroadcast the network nationwide in Venezuela, four hours a day, to the twenty-four million viewers at no cost to you. What a breath of fresh air your satellite could be to a country torn by crisis and in which every TV channel carries nothing but violence and conflict!"

How David and the mission president praised and thanked God for making such an avenue available. The Venezuela-Antilles Union voted to mobilize the entire church twice a month in sacrificial support of ADVenir. When God takes charge and displays His miracles, amazing things happen. How fast the entire world could be ready for the sound of the trumpet of King Jesus as He approaches the earth!

The Crisis

Strategic events regarding the Adventist Spanish Television Network (ADVenir) developed during March 2003.

First, ADVenir signed a five-year contract for satellite service with Intelsat 805. The Intelsat representative visited ADVenir from Washington, D.C. After he had seen the operation, he said, "I believe your format and content will place ADVenir at the top of Hispanic Christian broadcasting satellite networks. We will give you premium power and two months of service at no extra cost."

Second, ADVenir completed installing the satellite uplink facility, and a twenty-four-hour uplink to all the Americas and western Europe began in March 2003.

Third, ADVenir arranged two meetings—one with the administrators of the South American Division and one with leaders of the Bolivian Union—to explore avenues of working together to forward the church's mission.

Fourth, the final payment of $1.5 million (including interest) came due at the end of March 2003. The sellers continued to treat David and the ADVenir staff very kindly; their support for ADVenir's mission remained strong. But David understood that the sellers' financial needs made it imperative that the Adventists find some way to make the final payment.

The ADVenir team stood in awe. God was about to do something marvelous. They didn't know what He might do or where or when, but they knew He would never fail those who put their trust in Him.

Then at the very moment when ADVenir was about to go global with God's message of love to the Hispanic world, at the very time when

ADVenir was adding increased production and broadcasting costs, God saw fit to place its parent organization—Gospel Ministries International —in an extremely weak financial position. The constant flow of checks that had kept alive all of GMI's operations suddenly ceased. For the first time in seven years, the financial faucet just "turned off"! ADVenir suspended new-program production and used the last cash on hand to buy food for the workers. The stations remained on the air with prerecorded material. Mission planes also had to be temporarily grounded because of GMI's financial difficulties.

Why? David was impressed that this financial emergency must be of divine origin. After all, the organization's cash flow had always depended solely on God's providence. God was in control of the finances. Why, then, was He stopping them in their tracks? He must want them to pay attention. Well, they *were* paying attention!

Early that morning David prayed, "Precious Lord, if there is something we must correct, please reveal it to us. Millions of souls are at stake. Please let us know what needs to be done so that once again we may receive Your financial blessings."

After several hours of wrestling with the Lord, David received a growing conviction that God was saying, *"Before I can let you go on satellite full time, you need to make some important changes. Put your house in order!"*

The network board met together for several days. Each person examined his or her own life individually. When the group was assured that they were right with God in their individual lives, they took a close look at the operation of the network. They decided to make some needed organizational changes, including the addition of an experienced producer as a department head. Enthusiasm and peace ran high among the team at the studio.

Once again, they turned together in prayer to the Lord. "God, to the best of our abilities and consciences, we believe our house is now in order. We admit our total weakness and inability to care for our needs. We are totally dependent on You. With only a few days before the end of the month, we have three major needs to place in Your hands, Lord. First, if it is Your will that we continue on the air, we must pay our utilities and other normal bills.

"Second, although our satellite uplink is in place, we must pay our monthly deposit up front for satellite service.

"Finally, Lord, our kind sellers have waited so long for their funds. It seems they cannot wait anymore. Thank You for Your past care. Now we claim Your promise in Psalm chapter forty-six, verse ten:

> 'Be still, and know that I am God;
> I will be exalted among the nations,
> I will be exalted in the earth.'

"Since You have called upon us to 'stop,' we choose to 'be still' as the psalm says. We will not continue program production or uplinking pro-

The original master control room at ADVenir in Santa Cruz, Bolivia.

grams to the satellite until we see clear evidence that You will provide the necessary means to do so."

Many times before, God had chosen to answer prayer at the last minute. And so it happened again. Just three days before the end of March 2003, the *exact* amount of money needed to continue operations came in. Thrilled, the production staff set to work in earnest. Videotape began rolling.

> "It shall come to pass
> That before they call, I will answer;
> And while they are still speaking,
> I will hear" (Isaiah 65:24).

However, they still did not have the finances needed to continue the uplink to the satellite. The staff decided that they would wait for God's financing, just as they had with operations. In the meantime, David sent out urgent requests for much prayer on the critical issues pending. The eternal destiny of souls was at stake. David was sure that God would hear and answer prayer in His own time and in His own way. Their prayers focused on several crucial needs.

First, when David had last met with the sellers, he had nothing to offer except the possibility of letting them terminate the sales agreement. The funds that GMI had paid so far would be interest payments on the balance. But the owners had refused to terminate the sale saying, "We must go forward. Going backward would be a tremendous loss to both sides. But please plead with your God that He will provide the funds very soon."

Second, until God indicated that they begin uplinking ADVenir on a twenty-four-hour schedule, they must wait. Satellite rental was twelve thousand dollars per month; they must have divine confirmation before moving ahead in this area.

Third, the medical aviation programs and the schools in Guyana, Venezuela, and Peru had been blessed by God to spread the gospel in remote areas of the earth. All these programs needed special prayer and blessing at this time.

While they prayed and waited, God intervened. An envelope arrived with two checks from the same person. The note in the envelope read, "The Lord impressed me that my first check was not enough. Here is a second check for the same amount." Together, the two checks totaled twelve thousand dollars—exactly the amount needed for the first month's satellite rental!

On April 21, ADVenir began uplinking full time to all the Americas and western Europe on the Intelsat 805 satellite. Within days, responses began to pour in from viewers in countries in and around South America that were receiving ADVenir's signal. Truly our God is a miracle-working God!

In Venezuela, the Telecaribe television network began rebroadcasting ADVenir four hours a day during prime time to twenty-four million viewers in thirty-one cities throughout the country—free! The union communication director in Colombia reported that ADVenir was on nearly thirty cable networks. In El Salvador, the Adventist television station in Santa Rosa received permission to become the first affiliate ADVenir station. The Dominican Republic was making preparations to

The uplink dish for ADVenir. God has continued to bless the network with the equipment needed to broadcast His message to thousands across Bolivia.

downlink ADVenir for cable networks throughout that country. In Peru, a nationwide network of thirty-six station licenses was placed on the market for just under one hundred thousand dollars. Members there began praying that God would provide funds so that ADVenir could be rebroadcast throughout Peru. Pastors in Bolivia praised God for an ongoing increase in former Adventists returning to church and being rebaptized.

The day of miracles is not past. God is pleased to honor the faith of those who will step out and trust Him.

CHAPTER 12

Reflecting Light From Heaven

Meanwhile, at Colegio Gran Sabana in Venezuela, where Bob and Neiba Norton were based, a group of twenty-six people came in early March 2003 to build the hangar for the mission plane. The group also began laying blocks for Bob and Neiba's future home. Equally important, they raised money to buy the materials needed for both the hangar and the house. Bob gave a big thanks to Jeff Sutton, a student missionary, who arranged everything. When the runway was completed beside the school, Bob rejoiced. Until then, he had not been able to land the mission plane at Colegio Gran Sabana; instead, he had had to use the nearest airport, which was located at Santa Elena. This meant he had to walk almost two hours from the school to the airport each time he needed to use the plane. Now he could land right at the school. And he would not have to pay landing and parking fees at the Santa Elena airport. God's blessings were continuing.

The experience of working on these projects was a blessing also to those in the volunteer group who

The new hangar at Colegio Gran Sabana in Venezuela. Construction of a runway and hangar at the school meant Bob and Neiba Norton wouldn't have to walk almost two hours to and from the airport in Santa Elena.

had come for a few weeks to Colegio Gran Sabana. They saw the dedication of the students and the staff. They witnessed God's blessings on a daily basis. One college student in the group had tended to complain at first about all the inconveniences he was encountering on the project. As time passed, however, his attitude changed. Before returning home, he shared an experience that had made a significant impact on him.

Bob had invited this student missionary to go with him on one of his short flights. They landed on a terrible runway in a remote village to pick up an Amerindian husband and wife who had spent a couple months there sharing the gospel with the villagers. Both husband and wife wore old clothes and sandals, but they clutched a worn Bible like it was a treasure of gold. Bob had come to bring them back to their humble home near Colegio Gran Sabana so they could visit with their children, whom they had left behind to minister to the people of this village far out in the jungle. They planned to spend some time at home, working and farming in order to get some money and food so that they could return to that isolated village and continue telling the people of Jesus' love and soon coming.

"How often do you fly out and check on this couple?" the student asked Bob.

"Every month or so."

"Do they know the difference between a risky landing and a safe one?"

"Not really. It's all the same to them. They live in this primitive place for several months at a time. Just before they are ready to come home, I take the local pastor with me, and we have a big baptism. There's a good sized church group in that village now."

"How can they afford to do this? Who sponsors them and gives them supplies?"

"No one. They work extra hard while at home and save all the money they can. They even sell much of their garden produce. When they have enough money, they arrange for someone to care for their children and go again. When they run out of money and food, I fly out to get them so they can do it all over again."

During the rest of the flight this young complainer kept thinking of the couple's dedication to God and how they had surrendered their entire lives to service and were willing to risk all for God. He remembered, too, that Bob buys aviation fuel with his own money when donations don't come in. And he realized that for the last two weeks he had been grumbling about the "tough life" of working in the hot sun, getting dirty and tired, having only cold showers, and eating skimpy meals. He went back to college physically more tired than he left, but he felt refreshed spiritually, for he had caught a new vision of life.

Even during the fuel crisis in Venezuela, Bob continued to make emergency flights to take patients to the hospital and fly lay workers and pastors to their destinations. During this time there were about one hundred sick or injured people who would have died without Bob's help. Many baptisms took place due to Bob transporting pastors and laymen to share the gospel in remote areas.

Typical of Bob's experiences during this time was a twenty-two-year-old woman who lay seriously ill in a village where the runway had been abandoned for a long time. Termite mounds now covered most of the runway, and a gusty wind was blowing at thirty knots the day that Bob needed to fly into this village. He was able to find a stretch of the runway that was clear of the largest termite mounds, and he set the plane down, making his way around the smaller humps.

The villagers brought the sick woman, Maria, to the plane in a hammock. One look told Bob that without medical help, this woman didn't have much time left. Bob called Canaima, the closest town with a doctor. A half hour later, the doctor met his plane. "Please wait while I check her and see what's wrong," he told Bob. He returned a few minutes later to say, "Her appendix is ruptured; it probably happened yesterday. She will be dead in three hours if we can't get her into surgery. I'll go with you in case something happens on the way."

During the flight to the nearest surgical facility, the doctor could not get a pulse from the patient. Trying to save her, he injected medicine into her IV while in flight. Bob watched his tense face. After a few minutes he looked up and gave Bob a thumbs up sign. Bob knew then that the woman was still alive. As he flew, he prayed, "Lord, help us to get her there in time!"

Bob kept calling ahead so the airport would know where he was. An ambulance stood waiting for them. They quickly transferred Maria to the ambulance, and it sped off. The next morning the doctor met Bob at the airport. "Maria came through surgery and will make a full recovery," he reported. Bob thanked God for helping him get Maria to the hospital in time.

Still, the mission plane often sat in the hangar because there simply wasn't enough money for fuel. Yet, the needs continued. A pastor was stranded in a remote village, a lay worker had been waiting five days to return to the village where he worked, and several patients had been waiting for days to be flown out for medical help. The Nortons lived in a crowded rental house that often had no running water, and even when there was running water, they had to take cold showers because there was no hot water. Many times they turned on the light switch—and nothing happened. The phones seldom worked. The jeep was completely broken down, so they spent hours walking, for they had no money to repair the jeep or buy another one. Someone asked them, "Why do you put up with all this just to be a missionary?"

Bob and Neiba thought about that question. They knew that God had asked them to come to this part of Venezuela. He had appointed them to make a difference in the lives of the people there. Yes, there were difficulties. But life always has tough times. When they looked at the big picture and saw the many people who were hurting and sick, dying from malaria and other diseases, Bob and Neiba knew that due to God working through their efforts, these needy people now had a chance to recover and return home. They knew that God had called Bob to transport laymen and pastors to save souls who would never know a Savior without the contribution made by the mission airplane. And when they considered these things, they realized that for them, life truly was great! What a joy it was to know that God had put them at a special place to bring life, light, and hope to many. Cold showers didn't matter compared to serving the Master. The early church took the gospel to the world through sacrifice and suffering. Finishing God's work will require the same commitment.

Bob and Neiba smile and say, "We work for God, and that is enough."

In the United States, David Gates boarded a plane in Atlanta on his way to Walla Walla, Washington. He sat near a sharp-looking middle-aged gentleman.

"Excuse me, sir," the man said, extending his hand. "My name is Norman. I'm a colonel in the army. I'd like to tell you a story."

Surprised at his directness, David shook his hand and nodded. The colonel continued, "This morning as I stood in line at the gate to board the airplane, I looked down the concourse at the hundreds of passengers rushing in all directions. Some distance away, among the crowd, I noticed a particular man who caught my attention. I noticed something different about that person. His face was shining. I actually saw light coming from his face. I watched as he walked down the concourse and stepped in line behind me for this flight. After I took my seat, I kept watching for him to board this plane. Finally I saw him walking down the aisle and watched him sit down."

The colonel turned to look David in the face and said, "You are that person! What church do you belong to?"

Caught by surprise, David swallowed hard and managed to blurt out, "I'm a Seventh-day Adventist."

"Some of my best soldiers are Adventists, though I couldn't win a war with an army full of noncombatants." And he laughed.

As the flight neared its destination the colonel turned to David and confessed, "David, thank you for taking the time to explain your beliefs to me. Your total commitment to God is clearly written on your face. My estimation of Adventist beliefs has grown significantly today."

After his weekend appointments, David boarded the plane Saturday night for an all-night flight to Atlanta. Tired and looking forward to a few hours of sleep, he walked back toward his window seat in the rear of the plane, hoping he could rest. He had to step across a man and his wife who shared the adjacent seats with him. David saw them staring at him as he drew close. As he sat down, the lady blurted out, "You're a Christian, right?" David nodded and smiled as he fastened his seat belt.

"I knew it had to be the Holy Spirit," the lady spoke to her husband. Then she turned to David. "Sir, are you aware that you have light shining out of your eyes?"

David smiled, "It must be because this flight is a 'red-eye special.' "

"No, no!" insisted her husband. "When you got on this plane, both my wife and I noticed the light shining out of your eyes. We commented on it as we watched you walk down the aisle." David realized God had taken things in His hands and suspected there would be no sleep on his agenda that night.

"What church do you belong to?" asked the wife.

"I'm a Seventh-day Adventist," David responded.

"I'm so relieved! If you'd been from one of those churches that deny Christ, I'd have just died. I don't believe God would fill someone with His Spirit who doesn't believe this basic Bible truth."

David and his new friends spent the entire night discussing one Bible truth after another. Obviously these sincere Bible students just needed a bit of confirmation and encouragement to follow their newfound truths.

As David analyzed these two events, he realized how easily God uses the Holy Spirit to convict the minds of honest persons with truth. In both cases the Holy Spirit previously prepared the listeners to accept the truths before he spoke one word. Truly the Bible message will be carried not so much by argument as by the deep conviction of the Holy Spirit of God.

A few months later the leaders of the Southeast Venezuela Mission asked David to be a featured speaker at a Master Guide camporee. Becky and sons Carlos and Kristopher joined David in their assigned tent. The family was delighted at the opportunity to share their joy in committing themselves to God and mission service. They thrilled at the energy of almost a thousand youth spreading their light for God at the camporee.

On the second day, immediately after the closing prayer, a long line of young people waited to talk to the speaker. A man waited patiently until he could tap David on the shoulder. "My name is Luis," he said, "and I must tell you my story. I work as a scout for the Cleveland Indians baseball team in the United States and am deeply involved with church youth. Just before I left for this campout, I felt impressed to bring my checkbook. As I walked into this morning meeting, the Holy Spirit impressed me with the thought, *'When you see a man whose face is shining, write him a check for seven thousand dollars.'* When the meeting began, I was watching the people who walked onto the platform. Suddenly I noticed that the face of one speaker seemed to shine. I asked my wife if she noticed anything unusual, but she didn't. That man's face continued to shine throughout the service." Luis paused and pressed a check for seven thousand dollars into David's hand.

Just that morning David had prayed urgently for the money needed to pay the utilities for the Bolivian television network for that week. "Brother Luis," David said with tears of joy in his eyes, "how beautiful it is when God's people place themselves and their resources totally under His control. Obviously God longs to pour out His blessings on imperfect human beings to demonstrate His power to provide. All He asks for is our willing and total commitment. Truly God has honored your total commitment and faithfulness. May God bless you abundantly."

At the close of 2003, David praised God for His continuing protection for pilots Gary Roberts in Guyana, Bob Norton in Venezuela, and David himself. More than two thousand flight hours had been logged between them, and there had been no accidents or other dangerous incidents. Every hour was flown at no charge to those being served. They had begun the year with four planes and closed the year with six. The sixth airplane would be flown by Jeff Sutton to support the work in the jungles and savannas of eastern Bolivia.

Another evidence of God's blessing had been the issuing of a second permit for the Guyana Medical Aviation Service (GAMAS) to operate a recently purchased Cessna 182 with the capability for short takeoffs and landings. Except for the two permits issued to GAMAS, the government of Guyana has not issued permanent permits to any other church or missionary organization during the last thirty years! God be praised for the way His medical and educational work in Guyana has been accepted and appreciated within government circles.

God likewise blessed Kimbia Mission Academy and the Davis Indian Industrial College. Both schools in Guyana closed the school year operating at maximum capacity with an overflow of students.

In northeastern Bolivia, a beautiful 220-acre property with a winding creek that provided ample clear water had been purchased for a school. The fourth thatch-roofed house was nearing completion. It would serve as a cafeteria and meeting hall for students. Local church members seized an opportunity to purchase 280 neighboring acres of land by sacrificially raising three thousand dollars of their own money. They planned to open a lifestyle/healthful living center in the new area. Using a tractor, local workers prepared the land for the needs of the students and volunteer staff so that classes could begin on schedule in January 2004.

In the Gran Sabana region of Venezuela, Bob Norton reported that the response from village leaders was extremely supportive. One leader who was responsible for overseeing a large region of villages requested an evangelistic series. Bob promptly flew a lay pastor to the largest village in the area, and the meetings began promptly.

In all these areas of service, God continues to work miracle after miracle to honor the faith of His dedicated workers. In His strength, they are carrying out His command, " 'Let your light so shine before men, that they may see your good works and glorify your Father in heaven' " (Matthew 5:16).

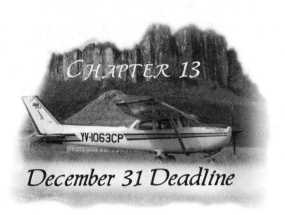

CHAPTER 13

December 31 Deadline

Due to a severely depressed economy in Bolivia, the sellers of the television network to Adventist Spanish Television Network (ADVenir) were forced to mortgage company assets and even liquidate personal assets to keep their businesses afloat. They advised David that they must set a deadline of September 25 for full payment of the remaining balance of the purchase price. They saw no way to extend the payment beyond this deadline. Accompanied by Don Johnson and Jenny Mendoza, his right-hand workers at the television station, David met with the sellers to discuss financial details.

The sellers reiterated their conviction: "We know God has given birth to this network. After you have made full payment for the network, we would like you to help us with programming on our other TV network, Red Uno, the largest in Bolivia. We want it to honor the Lord as does ADVenir." David agreed and then shared a ray of financial hope.

"A lady from the United States called with questions about our philosophy and our programming and financial situation. She expressed an interest in partnering financially with the network to resolve the outstanding debt. I understand she has a friend who also visited you and shared this information with you."

"Yes," the sellers agreed, "and after her visit, we chose to go forward in faith and continue waiting on the Lord to provide. We will extend the deadline for the final payment until the end of December."

A few weeks later Don Johnson was awakened at 5:00 A.M. by a call from the engineer on duty at the television station. Don heard a desperate voice say, "Water is rushing into our building. Come quickly!"

Looking out the still dark windows, Don could see pouring rain. Pulling on old slacks and a light shirt, he ran outside in a pair of rubber sandals. He slogged through two feet of water. When he got closer to the street, the water had risen waist-high—to the windshields of parked cars. Everything in the compound was covered with water.

Inside the building, Don waded through a foot and a half of water. Hundreds of new videos were floating around the programming room. David had brought them from the United States just a week before, and they had been stored on two lower shelves. The electrical power was still on, and the outlets sizzled and crackled as the water level reached them. Don had to turn off the power for safety's sake. Slogging around in the dark, he discovered eight very expensive editing computers under water. These computers housed huge banks of hard drives for video production. Things looked hopeless.

Don almost cried when he went to his office and found his laptop and digital video camera completely under water.

But God was not through working miracles. One by one, the large computers that had been under water became operational once more after a week of painstaking work—total disassembly, cleaning, drying, and reprogramming. The biggest loss was more than two hundred fifty completed video programs, many books that had been in boxes on the floor, and Don's laptop computer and camera. The flood had been a big setback, but the staff knew that God was still in control and that He would help them recover what they needed.

Because of the danger of electrical malfunctions and further damage to transmitters and other equipment, the staff decided to shut down broadcasting temporarily. During the flood, Don had watched as the water level rose on the amplifier cabinet outside under the huge uplink dish. This particular equipment had been provided by loving donors at a cost of one hundred thousand dollars. They simply couldn't afford to lose it.

Turning to one of the engineers, Don said, "We must hurry and broadcast a notice to our viewers that we will be off the air for some time. We have to shut down before any further damage occurs. As he quickly wrote the message to be broadcast, Don switched the "on air" monitor from channel to channel. ADVenir was the *only* local channel still broadcasting.

"Look, fellows," he said, "the Lord has kept us on the air so far. Maybe we should wait before broadcasting this notice and going off the air. It's a serious matter to shut down an international satellite signal affecting potentially millions of views in so many countries. Let's pray for the safety of our equipment and for the water to stop rising."

As they bowed in prayer, Don saw that the water was about four inches above the bottom of the uplink amplifier enclosure where equipment costing tens of thousands of dollars was housed. The water was also an inch above the base of the air conditioning unit for this equipment. Amazingly, after they prayed, the water began to recede quickly! Although the network advised its viewers that it might soon be off the air, the station never did shut down. Later, when Don opened the equipment door, he could see that the water had risen inside, leaving its mark less than one inch below the critical uplink amplifier! No matter how hard the devil tried to interfere with God's work, the Lord said, "Thus far, and no farther!" In the midst of the flood, God was there to work miracles. ADVenir's signal never left the air. Through the storm the air waves continued to carry God's beautiful message of peace and tranquility, bathed in inspirational music and accompanied by lovely scenes from nature. God, still in control, brought peace to the listeners.

For two weeks workers spread videos, cassettes, and books all over the studio to dry them out, hoping some would still be usable. The editing and production department went into full swing producing new material to put on the air as soon as possible. Jenny, the programming director, divided longer programs in half and added as much variety as possible with other materials that had escaped water damage.

Yet, more than ever, they trusted the future to the One who never makes a mistake and always cares for His own. God was leading them in the big challenges of recovering from the flood, and they felt confident that He would place the ministry on a firm financial foundation and help them find the professional staff of volunteers needed to produce quality inspirational programming for the Spanish world. They claimed His promise, " 'When you pass through the waters, I will be with you; / And through the rivers, they shall not overflow you' " (Isaiah 43:2).

In November the financial situation remained grim. The network business manager called David. "Come prepared to sign the necessary documents canceling our sales agreement. Our financial difficulties no longer allow us to continue waiting."

Everything pointed to imminent failure. Would ADVenir go off the air in Bolivia within days? Could they expect anything else? They had not been able to make any significant payments on the one-and-a-half-million-dollar debt in over eighteen months. But David had learned that the only way humans can predict the future is to look back to see what God has already done in the past. The record? Total success as God reveals His mighty arm in His own time.

During his morning devotions, David was convicted by the Holy Spirit to expand programming into other cities of Bolivia. Within two days of the time they would apparently have to close the network, David contracted with two engineers to install new downlinks and television transmitters in five large Bolivian cities. He wrote each engineer a check and thanked them for their willingness to move quickly. Sound illogical? Yes, especially at this time when only God could find a way out of their difficulties.

David's parents had gone to Venezuela for his ordination to the gospel ministry. Now, together in Bolivia, they went with David to the sellers' office.

"My personality and experience have always led me to be optimistic," David began. "God has blessed this network, which belongs to Him, with visibility, credibility, and worldwide success. However, He has not yet seen fit to provide the one and a half million dollars we owe you. You have been very patient and kind to us. Please know we will not misunderstand any action you must take. God knows what limits we humans have, and I know He will work within those limits. Please outline your requirements, and we'll comply with them."

Faces softened. The Holy Spirit could be felt in the room. "We know God owns this network and is doing our country a great favor," the sellers assured David. "Yet, we must pay our bills. Do you think that God might do something by the end of the year?"

"I know God will act as He sees fit. Please don't feel badly about setting a final date. Since I can't be back to Bolivia by that date, do you want to discuss what steps we should take if the deadline comes and we are not able to pay?"

One of the owners interrupted David just as the chief financial officer held out the contracts he had prepared for David to sign. Waving the papers away, he said, "No! Those will not be necessary. We will not discuss failure at all. God willing, that will never happen. We will deal with the problem only when we get to December thirty-one."

Tears welled up in David's eyes. Once again they knelt in prayer committing their lives and financial needs to their heavenly Father. They gave each other warm embraces as they left the office. The lawyer, sitting outside, seemed surprised at the peaceful, happy conclusion.

On December 23, with just eight days left before the expiration of the sellers' last deadline, during his morning devotions David read the story of Rebekah and her son Jacob. Jacob and Rebekah deceived Isaac in order to do things their own way. Instead of waiting for God to work things out, they gained only trouble and sorrow. David prayed, "God, I know the battle is Yours. I must be still and wait on You no matter what the consequences."

Just then the telephone rang, interrupting his prayer. The voice said, "I got up early and felt impressed to call you. I want to know more about your television network in South America."

David explained its history and told of God's blessings in the network's rapid growth. Then he explained the deadline he faced.

"How much do you owe?"

"One and a half million dollars. The interest over the last year and a half has eaten up the two hundred thousand we paid at the beginning."

"If you had to make a partial payment that would preserve the sale, how much do you think would be acceptable to them?"

"A half million dollars would be the minimum that I could think of offering them."

The voice spoke quietly. "I'll put a check in the mail today."

David's voice broke as he tried to speak. "Thank you! Thank you! God will be honored. His faithfulness is vindicated by this gift. Others will be inspired. The joy and benefits will last throughout eternity!"

"You're welcome. I will be in touch with you later after I contact my accountant. God bless." With that, the caller hung up the phone.

David and Becky cried and prayed together in gratefulness to God for His abundant mercies and faithfulness. That very day, David was scheduled to call the sellers in Bolivia with an update. But first, he placed a call to the network's business manager. "God has provided a miracle, just as you said He would," the manager said when he heard the good news. "I'm sure others will be encouraged to follow this donor's example and that the full balance will soon be paid off."

Later that day the donor called again. He explained that his wife had managed a business for forty years. Recently she had died, and her accountant had wanted to know what he should do with the proceeds from her business. That was when God had impressed the donor to call David the first time. However, when he had hung up the phone with David and called his wife's accountant to instruct him to write the check for five hundred thousand dollars, the accountant had become very upset. He was not at all happy about the decision to donate what had taken decades to accumulate through careful management. He urged the man to reconsider his decision. The donor asked David for some time to think about it.

For a couple of heart-stopping days, David and Becky hung on to God's promises and awaited the final outcome. Dozens of prayer partners asked God to rebuke Satan and intervene in favor of His work. The donor battled with his wife's accountant for several days to get access to his money. It took the power of Christ to break the enemy's grip on the money destined to save souls.

What a relief it was to receive word at last from the donor, who called and reconfirmed that he had not faltered in his decision to give. In fact, he had discovered that his wife had several other bank accounts. "David," he said, "I want to give the Lord the full amount as soon as I can receive legal possession of that money. Just keep praying." How everyone's hearts thrilled at God's goodness.

A friend called at this time to ask David about the television project in Bolivia. David told her briefly about the call he had received and the potential donation of a half million dollars. He added, "I believe God will send another five hundred thousand by year end."

"That's only a few days away. What makes you so certain?"

"My experience when I look back to what God has done in the past. During the past seven years our budget has doubled in size. As we have stepped out in faith, God has helped us to build schools, buy planes, and expand the broadcast work. In harmony with His promises, our donation income also doubled. Based on the past, I believe that God will impress someone to send at least a half million during the next few days."

His friend responded quietly, "According to your faith be it unto you."

Awakening at 4:30 A.M. on December 30, David spent time in worship and thanksgiving. Then he prayed, "God, I lay two burdens before You. Please take off our financial handcuffs for operating and equipment costs. At the moment, we have very little money for maintenance, utilities, food stipends for volunteers, subsidies for the schools, aviation programs, and equipment needs. Second, if it can be for Your honor and glory, please send an additional half million dollars so we can pay a significant amount on the TV station. This will double our budget for the eighth year in a row."

Suddenly the Holy Spirit interrupted his thoughts. *"Today is not the day I want you to ask for anything. Focus on your blessings. No requests, just thanks."* Peace and joy flooded David's mind as he sat in bed praising God.

"Thank Me specifically," the Sprit encouraged.

Slowly David began to understand. "God, I praise you for the entire one-and-a-half-million-dollar balance You will provide to pay off the television network. May Your name and faithfulness be honored as You show the world what a gracious God You are."

"Anything else?" he felt the Holy Spirit asking him.

"Well, Lord, I do need to pay off a few other debts, and we need money for operating expenses." Quickly he jotted down a few numbers. "Yes, I believe a hundred thousand dollars would be enough."

That day David went about his many tasks rejoicing in the Lord. With heavenly anticipation he waited to find out what God would do.

A friend asked David if he would be willing to take his grandsons for a short flight and share some missionary experiences with them. Always eager to inspire young people to work for God, David quickly agreed. While getting the plane ready for the flight, David received a call on his cell phone. His parents, who handled GMI finances, announced joyously, "David, your donor friend has the money in hand! The total from his wife's different bank accounts came to one and half million dollars! God has stepped in to save His network just twenty-four hours before the deadline that would force us to return it to the Bolivian owners!"

David's friend, who had asked him to take his grandsons on a plane ride, turned to them and said, "Boys, you have just witnessed a miracle that I hope you will never forget." Two hours later this friend placed an envelope in David's hand, stating, "My wife and I were so impressed by what happened today. We, too, want to be part of this miracle. After praying about it, we felt impressed to empty our bank accounts." Inside the envelope was a hundred thousand dollars—the additional amount David had requested from the Lord!

What a day of rejoicing that was! The family gathered together and with the psalmist they raised their voices in praise:

"Bless the LORD, O my soul;
And all that is within me,
bless His holy name!
Bless the LORD, O my soul,
And forget not all His benefits" (Psalm 103:1, 2).

"Oh, give thanks to the LORD!
Call upon His name;
Make known His deeds among the peoples.
Sing to Him, sing psalms to Him;
Talk of all His wondrous works" (Psalm 105:1, 2).

Together they knelt in prayer, humbly thanking God for so faithfully fulfilling His exceeding great and precious promises.

Nineteen months before, on June 5, 2002, David had written a check for the remainder of the debt with the agreement that the check should be held by the Bolivian network sellers until funds became available. Patiently they had done just that. Now prepared to pay them the entire amount, David called and asked them to quote the final payment, including interest.

They answered, "We reverently congratulate you for trusting a God who does answer prayer. You're right. With interest it comes to about one and a half million dollars. However, we'd like to show our support to God's television ministry. We've decided to donate back nearly one hundred thousand dollars in interest charges. We are willing to take the check you wrote over a year and a half ago for one point four million dollars."

Is God big enough to finance His work? Does He still work miracles? David and his family are eyewitnesses of God's power and care.

Many letters and comments have come to David asking, "Are you sure God is directing when you move ahead *before* you have any funds at hand? How do you differentiate between faith and presumption?"

David has answered with deep conviction, "God promises to direct us in the way we should go [see Proverbs 3:5, 6]. Also, Romans chapter twelve, verses one and two says that if we present our bodies a living sacrifice and are not conformed to this world but are transformed by the renewing of our minds, we can prove what is God's good, acceptable, and perfect will. These are God's promises, and we need to accept them by faith. Remember that God expects everyone to have faith, because without faith it is impossible to please Him [see Hebrews 11:6]. On the other hand, we also need to recognize that God may give special faith to some people as a gift, since faith is included among the spiritual gifts listed in First Corinthians chapter twelve.

"When we feel God's Spirit impressing us to do something that is in harmony with God's written Word, we should step out in faith and do it, praying that if somehow we have misunderstood His directions, we will not feel God's peace in our hearts [see Colossians 3:15]. After moving forward, we watch for God's confirmation through continued open doors or His providences. If we see evidence of that, we move forward with increased confidence. If we don't see that evidence, we ask God for further direction or correction. Many times Becky and I have prayed that if a project we are doing is not of God, that He will close it down. If it keeps going, then we have the confidence that it is God's project, not ours. This is one reason we do not ask for money. God will impress people to give if He wants that project to continue.

"There is a fine line between faith and presumption. That is why it is so important to know, with the help of the Holy Spirit, what God's Word says. The difference between faith and presumption is that faith leads to obedience of God's commands, while presumption excuses disobedience.

"Jesus trusted God's promises completely. He knew God's angels would bear Him up in their hands. But God had not commanded Him to jump off the temple. To do so would have been presumption. However, if God had commanded Him to jump off, and He refused, saying that He didn't want to tempt God, it would have been presumption not to believe and obey.

"There is an interesting, but sad, story in Numbers chapters thirteen and fourteen that deals with this very point. God led the Israelites through the desert to the border of Canaan. There He told Moses to send twelve men to spy out the land. When they returned, Caleb enthusiastically encouraged the people, ' "Let us go up at once and take possession, for we are well able to overcome it" ' [Numbers 13:30].

"Sadly, ten of the men contradicted him, saying, ' "We are not able to go up against the people, for they are stronger than we" ' [Numbers 13:31]. They went so far as to say, ' "Let us select a leader and return to Egypt" ' [Numbers 14:4].

"Joshua and Caleb pleaded with the people, ' "The land we passed through to spy out is an exceedingly good land. If the LORD delights in us, then He will bring us into this land and give it to us. . . . Only do not rebel against the LORD, . . . the LORD is with us. Do not fear them" ' [Numbers 14:7–9].

"The people refused to listen. In fact, they were ready to stone Caleb and Joshua. How disappointed and sad God must have felt, for He said, ' "How long will these people reject Me? And how long will they not believe Me, with all the signs which I have performed among them?" ' [Numbers 14:11]. Earlier, the Israelites had said, ' "If only we had died in this wilderness!" ' [verse 2]. God decided to grant their request. And when the Israelites realized that they had signed their own death warrants, so to speak, they suddenly changed their minds and decided to 'obey' God's order to go into Canaan.

"That, however, was no longer God's will for them. God told them to go back into the desert. Moses warned them, ' "Do not go up, . . . for the LORD is not among you" ' [Numbers 14:42]. Verse forty-four says, 'But they presumed to go up to the mountaintop.' [See also Deuteronomy 1:43.] Verse forty-five gives us the sad result, 'Then the Amelekites and the Canaanites who dwelt in that mountain came down and attacked them.'

"Read all of Numbers chapters thirteen and fourteen carefully and prayerfully. I believe God's children are again on the border of Canaan. Will we believe God's promises, hearken to His voice, and go forward by faith?

"We're living on the verge of eternity. God's people must learn now to trust Him intimately with even basic needs. Only then will we be qualified to carry this experience to the world. I have some suggestions for developing that experience of complete trust in God.

1. Start by placing yourself and all your assets totally in God's hands. They aren't yours anyway.

2. Focus your energies and investments on the mission of reaching people for God.

3. Allow the Holy Spirit to guide you into the privilege of risk to accomplish God's work.

4. When you see God at work, be it in your life or someone else's,

pray for and support it with your influence and resources. The growth of God's work at home is directly related to the support and growth of the work in the mission field.

5. Be flexible enough to allow others to develop their own way of working with God. Don't be surprised if He works through His children in other denominations.

6. God gave you the privilege of knowing and sharing the good news that Jesus is coming soon. This world is not our home. Give evidence you believe that.

7. Cling to the promises. Don't trust your feelings but only the Word of God. Remember to thank God for the rapid advancement of His work around the world."

The following incident demonstrates how God can reach down to change a life and a family.

Late one night, Offir lay on her bed with eyes wide open, unable to sleep. The daughter of a well-known physician in Upata, Venezuela, she saw her life as a complicated mess. Attractions of the world had weaned her away from the God she had known as a youth. With tears running down her cheeks, she cried out, "God, I've been gone from You so long. I'm not sure You would take me back even if I asked You to."

Several hours later and still wide awake, Offir decided to watch TV, thinking, *None of these stations can solve my problem. What I need is peace.*

Suddenly, there it was! A television program, *Moments of Peace,* appeared on her screen with beautiful nature shots and quiet sacred music. A sense of God's presence filled Offir's room with peace. She lay down on the couch to drink it in. Twenty minutes later fascinating scenes introduced another program, *It Is Written.* This program seemed familiar—world events, time to make things right with God, an invitation that drew her to Jesus in a white cloud, surrounded by millions of angels. Then came three angels with trumpets spinning around the world with the song, "Jesus Is Coming Again." The station, of course, was ADVenir.

Suddenly Offir pulled it all together. Her mind jumped back twenty-five years when as a young woman she had left the church. Now she knew God was calling her to make things right. The next morning she began searching for a local Seventh-day Adventist pastor.

When she found him, she blurted out her mission. "Last night I found an Adventist television station. I must be rebaptized this coming Sabbath." And she was!

Enthusiastically and joyfully she shared Christ with her family and friends. Her husband soon chose to be baptized. Together they praise God for their new life.

David and all the volunteers praise God that He has worked miracles to keep ADVenir on the air to continue to touch lives throughout Latin America.

Miracles Galore

God continued to bless the Adventist Spanish Television Network with new families of experienced volunteer workers. Joining ADVenir as director of the network was Pastor Remberto Parada, a Bolivian with thirty-one years of pastoral and administrative experience, and his wife, Flor. He brought with him the respect of church members throughout Latin America.

Another miracle that thrilled the staff came when Scott and Susan Grady and their two sons, Devin and TJ, joined the network staff as volunteers. Several weeks earlier David had been eating lunch with his brother, Doug. Doug and his wife, Brenda, are close friends of Scott and Susan.

"David, you know that Scott is looking for another job," Doug commented. "He has years of experience in broadcasting. Have you thought of giving him a call? I'd be willing to help him with his first three months of living expenses if he is willing to go work with ADVenir."

"Are you serious?" David was thrilled with the possibility.

"I certainly am," said Doug, handing David the phone. "Call him right now if you like."

When David explained why he was calling, Scott was speechless for a few seconds. "You won't believe this," he said slowly, "but just this Sabbath I went forward in church for special prayer. I poured out my heart to God, asking Him to show me where He wanted me to work. I believe He just answered me!"

Scott's professional experience of twenty years in broadcasting production made a difference in ADVenir almost immediately. The job he did as director of production, together with his multiple talents and language skills, blessed the listeners. Susan's creative enthusiasm, encouragement, and fun attitude added much to the volunteer families.

A third family to join ADVenir was Richard and Katie Carrera. Their involvement brought David and Becky great joy, for Katie is their oldest daughter. Scott described his impressions as he took his first tour of the network facilities in February 2004: "I could surely see that God was blessing this operation as I looked in amazement at some very basic equipment for a network as far reaching as this one. *How have they produced such excellent programs working with inadequate facilities?* I wondered. It certainly demonstrates God's power and leading."

Richard and Katie Carrera. They joined the group operating ADVenir in Bolivia. Katie is David and Becky Gates' oldest daughter.

God also blessed the Grady family with a third-floor furnished apartment located only one block from the television station and two blocks from a safe walking track, a clean bakery, and a fresh-fruit stand. All this was a tremendous help since they didn't have a car. It freed Scott to begin his work immediately. Very few volunteers start in such a comfortable, convenient place. Susan discovered that in Bolivia all cooking starts from scratch after buying the ingredients at the outdoor market. Her days filled up rapidly with homeschooling her boys, cleaning, cooking, shopping, and laundry. Language study occupied any additional time.

Within three weeks under Scott's guidance, the ADVenir production department produced several cooking programs, short spiritual segments for fillers, and youth programs. Scott also met Marco, a television-equipment representative, who helped him purchase new and used equipment at a remarkably low price.

At this time, the Venezuela-Antilles Union made plans for an evangelistic series in Barquisimeto with Pastor Stephen Bohr. David made arrangements to have it broadcast live on ADVenir, and a Brazilian engineer was hired to set up the equipment and to make sure the network was getting a good signal.

Becky and David arrived in Barquisimeto a few days before the meetings were to begin. Because all their friends already had guests in their homes, they decided to stay in a modest hotel near the auditorium. Saturday night the team worked almost until midnight finishing last-minute arrangements.

That night, as David tried to unlock the door of their room on the eighth floor, Becky noticed a man talking on a cell phone at the end of the hall. Suddenly the man began to wave wildly at them.

"Is that someone you know?" Becky asked.

David squinted. "Why, that looks like the Brazilian engineer. He was supposed to be traveling today. I didn't know he was staying in this hotel. Let me introduce you to him."

The Brazilian gave David a big hug. "Oh, Brother David," he exclaimed, "I believe this is a divine appointment. I didn't know you were staying in this hotel. I just happened to step out of my room to see if I could get a better signal on my phone. You are just the person I wanted to see. Please, step into my room. I need to talk to you."

As they went into the man's room, they immediately noticed that the TV was tuned to ADVenir. "I must tell you that I'm not only an engineer but the pastor of an evangelical church here in Venezuela. As you know, Brazil is mostly Protestant. Two years ago a large group of evangelical pastors began meeting together to plan ways to expedite the spread of the gospel in Brazil. Several of the pastors told of dreams in which God promised He would provide a Christian television station for them, but God showed one of these pastors that the television station would be started by a foreigner. They all pledged to support this network when it became a reality."

David and Becky listened with astonishment as the man continued, "I'm convinced God is taking the reins into His own hands in order to finish His work. We've researched several Christian networks, but none of them offered what we were looking for. Now that I've seen ADVenir, I've found the answer. Would you consider coming with me to Brazil to meet with some of these influential pastors? I'd also like for you to look at a television station that is for sale. If you decide to come and acquire the station, I know that many of the three hundred pastors will downlink and rebroadcast your signal within months."

Both Becky and David felt God wanted them to accept what could be an opportunity to reach the entire country of Brazil. Yes, they agreed, they would sacrifice their limited time together so that David could go to Brazil; it seemed so clear that God was opening a tremendous opportunity for them. As they knelt together in prayer, their Brazilian pastor friend kept thanking God over and over with tears. "Please God, don't allow anyone else to purchase that station till we get there," he prayed.

Becky and David went to bed that night sobered yet excited at seeing how God can lead His people to the finish line.

Two weeks later David left his small plane in Manaus, Brazil, and caught a commercial flight to meet with his pastor/engineer friend and his team. The group was immediately ushered into the mayor's office for their meetings. Together they knelt in prayer.

Then they explained to David that the full-powered television station for sale had the capability for unlimited repeaters throughout the country. Its tower and antennas, located on its own mountain-ridge property, overlooked five million viewers. "The cost of one point one million dollars includes a new five kilowatt transmitter," they concluded.

As he listened, the Holy Spirit impressed on David's heart the message, *"Don't leave this office without confirming the purchase."*

David spoke slowly and clearly, "I want to purchase this station. I feel impressed to proceed with the contract immediately."

Surprised but pleased they answered, "Another buyer has been aggressively pursuing the purchase. But he is still working on financing."

"Please understand that under God's direction, we will buy your station," David told them. "That means it cannot be on the market anymore."

"Yes, we understand clearly." They stood and shook hands on the deal. Less than a minute later a cell phone rang. It belonged to one of the owners of the station. The voice on the phone was from the other party interested in buying the station. "I've called to tell you that our group has the funds available to purchase the station. When can we arrange to close the deal?"

"I'm sorry," said the seller. "The station is no longer on the market. It has been sold."

The next four to five hours brought an avalanche of calls from important people around the city, begging the owners to reconsider their decision. They were even offered an additional two hundrend thousand dollars for the station. Finally, the owners turned off the phone.

What—or who—impressed David to confirm the purchase price immediately? God's miraculous power was seen once more at work.

David and the sellers drafted the contract over lunch. That evening, before David left town, the contract was signed!

It was the Holy Spirit who impressed David to use that golden moment to make a definite commitment to buy the station. The most fearful defeats and the most signal victories have often turned on a matter of minutes. God requires promptness of action.

David needed God to provide a solution for the one-hundred-fifty-thousand-dollar down payment within a few days. The sellers called with the news that the other interested party was offering a six-hundred-thousand-dollar down payment and were still trying to buy the station. If they did not receive the one hundred fifty thousand dollars within thirty-six hours, they would accept the other offer. Prayers flew heavenward. Within several hours God worked out a viable financing solution, and the owners received the money on schedule!

A few weeks later, in Santa Cruz, Bolivia, Scott and Susan Grady enjoyed special guests—the first to use their guestroom. David arrived in Santa Cruz with his two daughters and their husbands—Katie and Richard Carrera and Lina and Brad Mills. Katie and Richard arrived in Santa Cruz to use their talent at the network, while Lina and Brad, both RNs and pilots, came to join the new Technical-Industrial School in the northern part of Bolivia. Bob Norton, pilot of the medical aviation ministry in

Venezuela, flew down to Santa Cruz with them. Together the volunteers thrilled at his fascinating stories of flying in Venezuela's jungles.

After listening to Bob's experiences, Scott said, "We have miracles just as real in our asphalt jungles. Recently, ADVenir prevented a murder and suicide. A man planned to kill his family and then commit suicide. In order to cover up the noise of the pistol shots, he turned on the TV and put the volume at full blast. He heard beautiful music coming from the TV, and he stopped to listen. The music was followed by a message, and still he sat riveted to the television screen and what he was hearing and seeing. After the program, the Holy Spirit convinced him to put away his weapon and find out about a God who loved him. Today, this man and some of his family belong to the family of God. He is extremely grateful for the Holy Spirit's impressions that caused him to tune in to ADVenir."

Susan Grady added her own miracle story. "Our network office recently received a phone call from a well-known psychiatrist in the city who asked for a program schedule. He said that he and his colleagues have found ADVenir to be a perfect cure for tension and depression. They instruct their patients in group therapy to watch *Moments of Peace* nature videos accompanied by sacred instrumental music on ADVenir. They promise their patients peace if they will turn off all other TV stations and listen to ADVenir. Just as God used David's harp to keep King Saul sane, so the Holy Spirit's power relieves tension and depression today through sacred music and nature videos."

"Speaking of nature," Scott added, "God used a parrot to work another miracle.

"Whenever a family in Colombia listened to ADVenir, their pet parrot remained quiet. But if they turned to another station, the parrot made such a loud racket that they were forced to turn the dial back to ADVenir. When the parrot repeated this time and time again, they decided to pay closer attention to the programming that gave them quiet in their home. Day after day the family and the parrot listened to God's Word. Today, that family has chosen to be members of God's people."

"You all know about the miracle of the Brazil network," David said, smiling, "but you may not know that I flew to Belo Horizonte, the third largest city in Brazil, with no travel money except a credit card. No money, just an opportunity to reach five million people living in darkness with the gospel of hope. Yet, we were able to make the one-hundred-fifty-thousand-dollar down payment just two hours before the deadline. In a couple of months the remainder is due. Will God allow us to lose this million-dollar station? Never! However, in the last few weeks donations have dropped and remain at bare survival minimums. Giving requires personal sacrifice and risk. I'm pleading every day with God for victory over doubt. In faith I choose to trust His promises!

"Humanly we react to fear of failure and bankruptcy." David spoke slowly for once. "But we know fear doesn't come from God. When we give ourselves wholly to Him, He makes Himself responsible for the accomplishment of His work. By faith we must cooperate with One who knows no failure. Maybe God is allowing us to go through difficult financial times to see if we will obey and go forward depending on His power and exhaustless resources, realizing God is enough."

They sat in silence thinking. Then Scott asked, "You know, we're babes in trusting. We're new volunteers, who grew up with the philosophy of depending on our own funds, our own abilities, our own reserves. Be practical and tell us in simple words how we can develop a faith philosophy like that."

"Well, Scott," David answered, "first, we have to humble ourselves before God and guard carefully against temptation and known sin. Second, faithfully maintain a healthy prayer life and Bible study in order to hear God clearly. Third, move forward, accepting every opportunity He gives us, regardless of cost or risk. We must believe that what He has done for us in the past He will do again in the future. I am realizing that only as we move forward with unflinching faith in God's unlimited power to provide can we expect great things from Him."

Bob Norton spoke up. "That reminds me of Sven Gustavsen, the pastor/pilot in Norway. You told me how he felt the Lord convicting him to increase the effectiveness of his ministry by getting a helicopter so he wouldn't have to spend so much time driving those windy roads and waiting for ferries."

"Yes," said David. "One day he was looking through a magazine and saw a turbine-powered Hughes five hundred D. He felt God impress him that someday he would have that helicopter."

Sven Gustavsen, a pastor in Norway, used his own resources to build this small two-seater helicopter. The helicopter made his ministry more effective since he saved driving time and didn't have to wait for ferries.

"But first he used his own resources and donations from friends in the United States and Norway to build a small two-seater helicopter," Bob added.

"That's right," continued David. "He did what he could with what he had in his hands, and God blessed his ministry. He made such an impact in his area of Norway that he was featured in the national news. He was able to share with his countrymen, many of whom don't believe in God, his conviction that this project was of God. His helicopter was severely damaged when a hydraulic failure caused an emergency landing. But God protected him. He was

A hydraulic failure caused Sven to make an emergency landing and resulted in severe damage to the helicopter.

featured in the news again. The amazing thing is that the news reporters said they believed it was a miracle from God that Pastor Sven hadn't been hurt; one said she believed God would perform another miracle and help him get another helicopter.

"Shortly after the accident Sven called me on

the phone and said, 'David, I believe that your experience can be mine. I'm determined to do all in my power to locate a helicopter and negotiate with the owner before expecting God to provide the finances.'

"Pastor Sven searched the Internet and found the same kind of helicopter he had seen years before in the magazine. When he called the owner in Indianapolis, the man said flatly, 'It's not for sale—but I'm willing to sell it to you! You're welcome to come see it and fly it.'

"So Sven purchased a ticket to the United States even though he lacked the funds for a down payment on the helicopter. When he called me, my dad and I made a short hop by plane and went with him to see that gorgeous Hughes five hundred D helicopter. He'd found the right machine, all right. It had the power and smoothness to handle the rough and gusty winds of Norway's fjords. The owner listened to our stories of faith and God's deliverance and said, 'I'll sell it to you for five hundred fifty thousand dollars.' We prayed together and left for the airport. Only a miracle from God could put such a powerful evangelistic tool into our hands. We left with joy and peace knowing we had done our part. The ball was now completely in God's court. Would we see Him swing into action? Would God work a miracle to allow Pastor Sven to buy a five-hundred-fifty-thousand-dollar helicopter?

"Two days later, a friend called me about the helicopter.

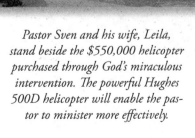

Pastor Sven and his wife, Leila, stand beside the $550,000 helicopter purchased through God's miraculous intervention. The powerful Hughes 500D helicopter will enable the pastor to minister more effectively.

I wondered how he knew about it. Then he said, 'Please call another friend of mine.' I did, and that friend asked me many questions. Finally he said, 'I've been in Norway, and I have a special place in my heart for God's work there. Recently I received an unexpected eighty thousand dollars. I want the entire amount to go toward the purchase of this helicopter.' "

Scott grinned. "I think I'm beginning to be a part of the 'trusting volunteer gang.' In my letters I've mentioned our need for audio equipment for the studio and control room. I just received an e-mail from a reader who decided to take on the project. She made many calls to her family and friends and raised almost all the money needed for that project in one morning! What a blessing that will be when we begin purchasing this equipment next week. This gift has certainly increased my faith. I know God is able to provide for our needs at ADVenir."

God doesn't waste time. He loves to place tools in the hands of His children so He can use them to finish His work. Ellen White has written, God "is well pleased when they [His children] make the very highest demands upon Him, that they may glorify His name. They may expect large things if they have faith in His promises" (*The Desire of Ages*, p. 668).

CHAPTER 15

Hurricane Ivan, Bandits, and Prisons

For John and Sue Bartels and their children, the great day—March 29, 2004—had come. "Just think, John!" Sue smiled from ear to ear. "Today we finally have a home here in Grenada! It may be only a third the size of the home we sold, and we may have spent every penny we have, but I love our little two-bedroom apartment. I know God is leading us."

"I'll be even happier when renovation of the TV station is completed," John replied. "God willing, we'll have that done by August."

But on September 7 Hurricane Ivan struck! Category 4 winds and rain devastated the entire island of Grenada—fallen trees, broken power lines, almost every house without a roof. The hurricane

The Bartels family stand in front of the TV station in Grenada following the destructive hurricane of August 2005.

ripped off the roof of the Bartels' apartment and nearly completed studio, drenching everything. For weeks after the hurricane Sue and John spent long hours from dawn to dusk, sweeping out water, drying out various items, cleaning, and fighting the ants and hornets that had lost

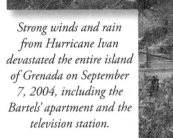

Strong winds and rain from Hurricane Ivan devastated the entire island of Grenada on September 7, 2004, including the Bartels' apartment and the television station.

their homes and were trying to move into the Bartels' home.

John and Sue constructed a temporary roof, put up tarps, and packed what belongings they could salvage. With no drinking water or electricity in the building, life became extremely difficult. Hauling water was a constant chore. They felt fortunate if they got more than a couple of showers a week. Wholesome food was scarce. After more than three weeks of this hard work, they felt emotionally and physically drained.

Then on September 30, Gary and Wendy Roberts flew to Grenada and rescued them. What a blessing it was to be together on the island of Margarita, just off the coast of Venezuela, for a few days of rest and relaxation. They enjoyed the fellowship of friends, relaxed on the beach, walked through the mall, ate good food, prayed, studied God's Word, and enjoyed long naps. They hadn't realized just how exhausted they were. Over and over they thanked God for putting this idea into Gary's and Wendy's hearts.

Then they flew to Guyana, hoping to get good-quality lumber to reconstruct the television studio in Grenada. They spent several days drawing designs for a new roof and estimating needed materials and costs. Purpleheart wood, very strong and durable, cost much more than John planned.

Should he buy cheaper wood? The morning that he would need to make a final decision, he studied Luke 6:48, 49 for his worship. In these verses, Jesus talks about building on a solid foundation. Was God directing him not to compromise the integrity of the new roof? Could God, who knows the future and the strength and force of a hurricane, be speaking to him? John shared his thoughts with Sue. After more prayer, they listened to the Holy Spirit's impressions and ordered the strong purpleheart wood to rebuild the house and television studio. John and Sue had only about half the money to buy the wood, but they stepped out in faith, trusting God to provide.

John and Sue had to return to Grenada on October 19 before the lumber was delivered. When they arrived home, they saw with dismay that the tarps they had put up had not kept out all the rain. Their home looked like a swimming pool filled with critters. Where could John, Sue, and the kids find a place to rent? They called a friend to see if one of his apartments might be available for a few days. How happy they were to hear him say, "Come on over. You can stay as long as you need to!"

"God is so good!" Sue exclaimed. Their temporary home had water, electricity, a phone, Internet, and best of all—a roof!

To top off God's blessings, the day before they needed to pay for the lumber they had ordered in Guyana, John got an e-mail from David, "All the funds you need are available and have been transferred to Gary's account so that he can complete the lumber transaction for you in Guyana." God had worked another huge miracle for John and Sue!

On Friday, October 29, Gary Roberts received notice that the lumber was ready for him to load into a container for shipment to Grenada. Gary took Dave Hossick, an ADRA volunteer from Canada, to help load the heavy wood. Dave comes every year to help in thousands of ways in Guyana. His willing, happy attitude lifts many burdens for the missionaries.

The two men spent a busy morning trying to get all the customs papers and shipping documents completed. As they walked from the shipping company to the lumber store—about two hundred yards—Gary explained to Dave, "We'll load seventy sheets of plywood plus the purpleheart wood. I have to pay in cash. In this bag is about ten thousand dollars. That will cover the cost of the wood and the shipping fees with enough left over to pay my fuel bill for the plane this month. I don't like carrying around so much money in cash, but I have no choice this time."

Suddenly someone grabbed Gary in a headlock from behind. He couldn't breathe. At the same time, another hand grabbed his wallet and

tried to remove his belt in order to steal his palm pilot. A third person started a fist fight with Dave. Right then, Gary wasn't as concerned about his wallet or the palm pilot as he was about the fact that he couldn't breathe!

The three bandits, armed with knives and pepper spray, suddenly released Gary. He turned to chase them as they rode away on bicycles. He had

Dave Hossick with helpers Jacob and Shadrack. Dave spends time every year as a volunteer missionary in Guyana, carrying out a multitude of tasks to further the work of God.

almost reached the man who had held him, when he realized that he had only one free hand—he was still holding the bag that contained the ten thousand dollars! His passport was in his other hand.

Gary and Dave continued chasing the bandits, shouting, "Thief! Thief!" Everyone nearby, including the security guards, basically ignored what was happening. Fortunately, the thieves didn't take anything from Dave. He wasn't carrying a wallet, and they didn't try to take his passport or his money belt, which contained a significant amount of money.

Both men were unharmed. True, Dave's face showed marks of his attacker's fist, and Gary's neck was very sore. His voice sounded like he had been a chain smoker for fifty years. But the men praised God that the thieves seemed blinded to the bag of money and Dave's money belt, which was a usual target. Gary lost his palm pilot and about two hundred dollars. He lost his driver's license, pilot's license, and airplane mechanic license. Gone, too, were his wife's driver's license and nursing license. And all his credit cards had also been taken.

God's hand must have covered the money bag, for the thief had to push it aside to get at Gary's wallet. As Gary and Dave loaded the wood, both men kept repeating the promises of God—like the one in Psalm 91:15:

> He shall call upon Me,
> and I will answer him;
> I will be with him in trouble;
> I will deliver him and honor him.

The good news was that they got all the shipping and customs documents done and the container loaded before sundown. Normally this process could take more than three days. Gary had to fly into the interior of the country the following week, so Friday was the only day he could care for shipping the lumber. Truly, humans can do nothing by themselves, but with God all things are possible. Satan tries to destroy us and God's work, but God's power is stronger than Satan's. Just ask Gary and Dave.

Back in Grenada, progress crawled. Because of all the damaged buildings from the hurricane, construction workers had more jobs than they could handle. Most businesses had also suffered damage to their facilities and were not operating at full capacity. Phone lines were still down, supplies were scarce, and workers of all kinds were overwhelmed with requests for their services. In light of all this, John and Sue, with the help of two friends, struggled to tear down the damaged portions of their home and the television studio. They worked hard to remove what was left of the ceiling and all the wiring in the building they had spent so much effort building just before Ivan struck.

By the middle of January 2005, John and Sue were ready to hire a civil engineer to redesign the television station/studio. The first drawing, which had been done by hand, couldn't adequately convey all the details that needed to be addressed. They also needed a mechanical engineer for the studio's air-conditioning system and an electrical engineer to complete the electrical design and draw the plans according to Grenadian codes. Each time they stepped out in faith and hired a professional to assist with the design work, the Lord supplied the necessary funding—keeping His promise to provide for all their needs "according to His riches in glory by Christ Jesus" (Philippians 4:19).

Despite John's and Sue's best efforts, however, the project kept dragging along, frustrating them repeatedly. Design tasks that should have taken only a few days or weeks took months. Could God be giving them a special gift of patience? They clung to His promise,

> Wait on the LORD;
> Be of good courage,
> And He shall strengthen your heart;
> Wait, I say, on the LORD! (Psalm 27:14).

By May 2005, all the designs, reviews, and corrections to the structural and architectural drawings for the TV station/studio, satellite up-link enclosure, and parking area had been completed. The plans included provision for a radio station, located below the parking area, to be operated by the local conference. Licenses for the radio station were verbally approved in April.

No rebuilding had actually begun by June 2005. The building was still in ruins. Meanwhile, eight thousand dollars' worth of hardwood from Guyana and other building materials were stored in the remains of the small studio with tarps covering the roof. The regional communications authorities had given verbal approval for John and Sue to broadcast via satellite, but they were still waiting for written approval from the Grenadian government. But God has perfect timing, and His plans to spread the gospel in the Caribbean will succeed.

While they waited, design work on the broadcast system progressed, and God continued to pave the way by leading John and Sue to find a supplier of broadcast equipment who would save them about twenty thousand dollars compared to the supplier they had intended to use. Now they began waiting for God to provide the funds to pay for all the equipment and rebuilding. They believed that God would care for the finances, too, at just the right time. They knew that He would make it possible for them to share His love throughout the Caribbean islands.

Meanwhile, in Georgetown, Guyana, Gary and Wendy Roberts continued to hope and pray that they could move from their small upstairs apartment near the hospital. They longed for a home in the country, away from the hot, noisy city and near a hangar and an airstrip where Gary could do maintenance on the airplanes, which would save him time and money. Unfortunately, the airport he was using allowed maintenance work only on Sundays and holidays when the hangar wasn't in use. Gary had the added inconvenience of having to transport his tools back and forth between home and the airport, which was both time consuming and extra work for him.

Eventually, they found an airstrip that hadn't been used for years. It was located in the country near the town of Bethany, only twenty-five minutes by air from Georgetown. Gary and Wendy rejoiced. Here they could be accessible to Georgetown but still follow God's counsel to live in the country.

Another plus was the proximity of the proposed Medical Missionary Training School, with Gilbert and Melissa Sissons in charge. They planned to open the school by September 2006. This school would further train the graduates of Kimbia Mission Academy and Davis Indian Industrial College in the areas of health and evangelism. With a baby due in June, Gary and Wendy felt a move from Georgetown was urgent.

Gary continued to fly to the same villages David Gates had initially been serving, but his range had also expanded tremendously in the three and a half years he had been in Guyana. He had placed Bible workers in several new villages and had plans to place more soon.

About a year and a half earlier, representatives from a village had come asking for help. The village had no airstrip and no radio, and the villagers had to walk four hours to the nearest source of medical help. Gary told them that if they would build an airstrip, he would be able to begin conducting clinics in their village. So, the villagers built a very short runway, and Gary and Wendy started conducting clinics there using their nursing skills. They placed ham radio equipment in the village.

After that Gary answered several calls for persons in that village who needed emergency medical treatment. As a result of the medical work, the villagers asked for someone to teach them of a loving God. A family who had completed Bible School training in Paruima responded to the plea and agreed to carry the gospel to this village. In March 2005, Gary had the joy of flying a pastor to that village to baptize ten people who had chosen to follow Jesus!

Another dedicated Bible worker felt impressed that God wanted him to come to two strong Catholic villages, Itabac and Kanatang. The headman in each place stated firmly, "We do not want your religion, but we have a problem. We have only one teacher in our government school. It's impossible for one teacher to care for all sixty students in the various grades. Please could you supply us with a good teacher for our children?"

This was a call to sacrifice. Housing was limited in both villages. There were no good water sources. The teachers would need to start a small farm to grow food to support themselves while they taught. Were there trained Amerindians who would respond?

Gary presented the challenge to the Bible workers in Paruima. One worker volunteered, saying, "I am committed to spreading the good news of Jesus. What better way to reach suspicious people than through their children? The Holy Spirit will guide me what to say and do. God will supply my needs." At Kimbia Mission Academy the same thing happened—an individual volunteered to accept the challenge. Now each village has dedicated teachers who pray for tact and skill to instill in the minds of the children a love for God and a desire to do His will.

Gary and Wendy thank God for willing, committed Amerindian Christians. God doesn't force people to work for Him. These volunteers consider it a privilege to serve, not a sacrifice.

In Santa Cruz, Bolivia, Scott Grady continued to meet challenges in connection with the television network. And they continued to witness miracles that increased the faith of all those connected with the network. Twice within a single month they faced equipment problems that took them off the air. The second time was on a Friday morning. The equipment technicians explained, "A piece of uplink equipment needs replacing. Nowhere in Bolivia can we buy or rent one. We'll have to send to the United States, which will take time. However, we'll remove the defective part, try to find the problem, and hope to repair it. But don't count on it."

While the technicians worked, Scott and his staff prayed. Meanwhile, ADVenir was off the air. Just as Scott was telling the master control operators that they wouldn't need to come to work until Tuesday morning, the technician showed up, "I found the problem," he said. "And I was able to fix it using parts from two old pieces of equipment lying around the shop. I'll install it, and we'll be on the air within an hour."

Does God still perform miracles for His people? The television team knelt together to praise God that the gospel message would be beamed halfway around the world to the Americas and into Europe on that Sabbath day.

CHAPTER 16

Culture Shock Adjustments

When Brad and Lina Mills (David and Becky's son-in-law and daughter) arrived in Guayaramerin, Bolivia, they were met by two faithful volunteers— Samuel Becerra, a Bolivian doctor, and Rosa Yungure, a Peruvian teacher. Both had been working hard, with the help of local church members, to create a new school. The locals had lovingly named this school the Richard Gates Technical Industrial School in honor of David's father, who had worked as a missionary in this part of Bolivia.

It was amazing to see how much progress had been accomplished. Not long before, David and Becky had spent a weekend in Guayaramerin due to an error on the part of an air traffic controller. While there, they had visited the local Adventist church and were met by thrilled church members who remembered David as a child. They begged him to restart the missionary work in their area. Some land was donated, and work began.

The early stages had not been easy. The donated land was thick, overgrown jungle that was difficult to clear. But thanks to the support of the local founding school board members and several months of back-breaking labor by Peruvian volunteer Ytler Sanchez and his team, enough land was prepared so that Brad, Lina, and student missionary Andy Hanson could plant gardens and erect several huts when they arrived. They fastened their hammocks to the rafters of the huts and joined the working crew.

One evening Brad and Samuel chartered a truck to bring needed supplies to the school. It was the rainy season, and the road was not paved. As a result, the truck became stuck at the entrance to the school. All the missionaries worked until 3:00 A.M. trying to push the truck out of the mud. Finally, they unloaded the truck, carrying mattresses, stoves, water tanks, and other supplies—by hand—for a mile through the dark jungle until they reached the school. Exhausted, Brad and Lina tossed their newly acquired mattress to one side and fell asleep in their hammock. That very night the hammock broke, and both Brad and Lina fell to the floor. If only they had slept on their new mattress!

Through God's incredible power, school began in a little over a month after Brad and Lina arrived in Guayaramerin. Twenty-five excited boys and girls came to learn of God in that new school. Though the majority were not Adventists at the beginning of the school year, by the end of the year every student had given his or her heart to God and had been baptized!

Brad and Lina worked with Dr. Samuel to start evangelistic medical work in a nearby jungle village where the light of God's love had not yet penetrated. They used medical work to build relationships with the people and then shared Christ's love with them. Toward the end of the first year, they held a large evangelistic series of meetings in the little village of El Yata. The held clinics during the day and encouraged the people to come to the meetings each evening to hear medical lectures and the preaching of God's Word. They were amazed at the attendance; each evening more than ninety persons came to the meetings. And the end of the series, El Yata had its first Seventh-day Adventist baptismal service. Seven individuals chose to give their hearts to the Lord and be baptized.

Upon returning from a trip to the United States, Brad and Lina were accompanied by Brad's younger brother, Bryan, and newlyweds Jeff and Fawna Sutton. The long journey began in Miami on September 2, 2004; the group finally arrived at the Richard Gates Technical Industrial School

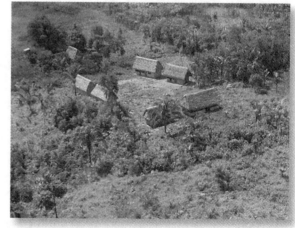

An aerial view of the Richard Gates Technical Industrial School, Guayaramerin, Bolivia. The school is named for David Gates' father.

on the evening of September 9. Part of the trip included a thirty-five hour bus ride that wound up to sixteen thousand feet on a narrow dirt road. The ride was beautiful but scary. The group looked down thousands of feet to the bottom of valley below, knowing that Jesus was there to hold the bus on the narrow track.

At the school, located deep in the jungle, they thrilled at the colorful butterflies, birds, and flowers—and the absence of traffic noise. No house was immediately available for Jeff and Fawna, so Brad and Lina invited them to live in their empty kitchen. Water from the creek provided for all their needs—drinking, bathing, and cooking. The snakes hiding in the grass along the path made it dangerous to go for water after dark. In the nearby town they could buy all the ingredients for a perfect lunch. There were avocados, onions, garlic, bread, and lettuce. And there was fruit in season. Otherwise, rice and beans formed their staple food. Jeff spoke Spanish, but Fawna struggled to communicate.

Their daily prayers included a plea for volunteers to replace Brad and Lina, who would be leaving in December to continue their studies. Jeff, a pilot, planned to serve on the Bolivian Aviation and Medical program. Fawna, a nurse, would help out in the hospital in Guayaramerin. She hoped to begin midwifery training and prenatal and postnatal check ups for the mothers. Presently, babies were delivered by older women who had no training. Fawna was hoping to work with the

Students in the girls' dormitory at the Richard Gates Technical Industrial School, Guayaramerin, Bolivia.

doctor who ran a clinic at El Yata, five kilometers from the school. This clinic had neither electricity nor running water, and during the week the doctor worked only from 8:00 A.M. until noon. Lina, Brad, and Fawna, eager to use their nursing skills, made a trip to El Yata to see the doctor. While they were waiting for her to arrive, a man rushed up to the clinic carrying a crying child. The little girl had a large open cut on her head that needed stitches. Brad took the motor bike to the school to get some local anesthetic and suture materials. He returned with the doctor, whom he had found at the school. They all watched the doctor struggle to push the needle through the tough skin on the child's head while they tried to hold the screaming, frightened, little girl.

While all this was happening, a woman walked up who was five months pregnant. She had pain in her abdomen. Lina and Fawna checked her and her baby; they found she had a urinary-tract infection, which could cause early contractions if not treated. The doctor ordered some antibiotics and told her to drink lots of water.

Surely God's hand had directed them to be at the clinic when others needed help. They remembered God's promise,

> Trust in the LORD with all your heart,
> And lean not on your own understanding;
> In all your ways acknowledge Him,
> And He shall direct your paths (Proverbs 3:5, 6).

Not only did the Suttons need a house, but the school needed materials to build two classrooms. Students had to be turned away because there was no room. Unfortunately, many of the local people thought the gringos should supply the money and do the work. How could they help the people understand that they needed to work for their own school? It was a problem demanding wisdom from God. Jeff invited the local church members to help him haul sand to make cement blocks. About ten men showed up Sunday morning. The trail to the sand, about four hundred yards away, started out high and dry. Then came a section of slippery muck with big roots one had to step over. Next came a log bridge across the river, and then a small hill.

Jeff proposed, "I think the man who can carry more than the gringo ought to have a prize." Everyone laughed, sure that one of them could beat him. But Jeff knew that because of his long legs, each of his strides would equal almost two of theirs. He worked hard, walking fast and singing as he worked.

By lunch time they were all exhausted, but happy. Not only had they accomplished much, they had a new respect for this hard-working, vegetarian gringo, for none of the men had beat Jeff!

Encouraged by this positive response from the people, Jeff invited the church members to come to the school and work again the next Sunday. This time twelve men came to help even though it was raining. Some of the men worked on the farm. The rest helped on the Sutton's house. By the end of the day, part of the framing for the house had been erected. Four huge poles for the main structure and all the poles to make the roof were in place. Fawna, who had taken the two student missionaries to town that day, was ecstatic to see so much progress on her future home when she returned.

Both student missionaries from Southern Adventist University were training to be nurses. Like most newcomers from civilization, they suffered from major culture shock at the primitive living conditions. "Remember," Fawna warned them, "everyone who comes to a situation like this goes through a period of not wanting to stay. First, you miss your family. Second, everything seems strange and wrong. Getting used to unusual foods, lack of conveniences, lots of bugs and snakes—all these make life tough. You're tempted to quit and long to take the next plane to the States. Tell Jesus how you feel, study His life in the Gospels, and help others. Stick it out, and you'll be forever thankful you did."

At this time Jeff received word that he would soon be able to take the necessary training and flight tests needed to fly the mission plane in Bolivia. David arranged for the use of a plane in Trinidad, Bolivia. So, early in November the Suttons began a long twenty-four-hour bus ride. They hoped to stay with one of David's aviation friends in Trinidad.

In Trinidad, they found a temporary home with a family who owned a large German Shepherd dog. He liked to play with Jeff but showed no friendliness to Fawna. Soon after they arrived, Fawna went into the yard one evening to take the clean clothes off the line. The dog sat next to the door playing with a ball. As Fawna neared the dog, he growled. She jumped back. He lunged at her and began biting her arms. She screamed, but he continued to attack her. It seemed like an eternity to her before the daughter of the family came and stopped the dog. Jeff quickly took Fawna inside and put water on her throbbing arms. Fortunately, she had only bruises and four painful puncture wounds.

Fawna was thankful that the dog had not attacked her face or neck and that he hadn't broken any bones. "Thank You, God," she prayed, "for Your protecting care." She was grateful, too, that the family would now keep the dog tied.

Volunteers Matthew and Julee Smith, working in Guyana, also suffered from culture shock. They arrived in Georgetown August 26, 2004. No one met them when they arrived, so they took a taxi to Gary and Wendy's apartment near the hospital. There was no one at home. Three hours later they found someone who could let them into the apartment. They were tired, hungry, and suffering from jet lag. Coming from the cool weather in Calgary, Alberta, they were feeling the effects of the hot, humid atmosphere in Guyana. And they could find nothing to eat in the apartment.

The kind hospital administrator took them to the open market to buy food. When they returned to the apartment they received another "welcome." A frog was sitting in the bathroom sink! As they took a walk along smelly ditches, toads started jumping out of their way, and colorful parrots screeched from the treetops. All in all, it was quite an introduction to a new culture for Matthew and Julee. That night before their exhausted bodies flopped into bed, Matthew opened his Bible. "Julee, we're in God's hands. We must trust Him to carry us. He's promised to be with us wherever we go. We need to believe His promise."

Matthew and Julee spent the next few days cleaning Robert and Wendy's apartment and exploring this hot, strange, dirty city. Gary and Wendy arrived back home on September 1, and two days later Gary flew Matthew and Julee 150 miles into the jungle, where the couple joined the Amerindians in the village of Paruima. Their task? Working with the students at the Davis Indians Industrial College (DIIC).

What an incredible flight over dense jungles, winding rivers, and many waterfalls! Gary circled the village. They saw the white church on the hill. He gave them a bird's eye view of the nearby campus before they landed.

Matthew and Julee Smith eating with the students in the cafeteria of the Davis Indian Industrial College, Paruima, Guyana.

Friendly village people quickly paddled their dugout canoes on the black waters of the Kamerang River to the airstrip. Climbing up the steep bank, many held out their arms in welcome. Most could speak some English.

The new volunteers enjoyed the dugout canoe ride from the airstrip to the campus. There was beauty everywhere: gorgeous birds flying from the tall trees and orchids hanging like bouquets designed by the master Florist!

They landed by a huge, smooth rock, the boat dock to DIIC. The Amerindians had no trouble pulling the suitcases and boxes to the top of the rock, but Matt and Julee faced a challenge juggling luggage while not slipping back. At the top of the dirt stairs children smiled shyly, standing by a hand-painted sign, "WELCOME TO DIIC."

The local people took them up the stairs of the new Health-Science building on the campus. The second floor consisted of four large new rooms with thin walls that did not go up to the roof. There was no other housing available, and Matthew and Julee would be sharing this space with another couple and their ten-year-old son, as well as another man. Privacy is not a high priority among the Amerindians.

Six days later five student missionaries, three young men and two young women, arrived. They would teach and work with the students. Together they visited the friendly, beautiful people in the village, worshiped with them on Sabbath, and enjoyed a jungle hike up Rain Mountain where they reached the springs that provide pure water for the school. Long plastic pipes, placed to take advantage of the steep mountain slope, provide water pressure for each building at DIIC.

Everyone kept busy cleaning up the campus, painting the boys' dorm, cooking, and harvesting peanuts. A local man came to Julee. "We announced to the villagers that we need help harvesting peanuts. They're getting overripe and sprouting. The villagers will work all Sunday morning and expect lunch for helping. Could you please plan lunch for them?"

"All we have is rice. We could dig up *tanya* and *eddo* [something like a potato], and also make green papaya curry and beans. Is that enough?"

He smiled. "That will do fine. We eat very simply here with what we can grow or harvest from the jungle."

School began on September 20. Matthew handled the administrative tasks as director of the school, plus teaching Bible II and math. He loved being the spiritual leader. Julee taught health classes, helped with the choir, and functioned as the staff social coordinator. She also worked as school nurse and helped with the cooking. The staff continued to harvest peanuts. Adam, one of the student missionaries, started to pull up a peanut plant and grabbed onto a big green caterpillar with spine-like protrusions all over its body. These produce a poisonous sting causing severe pain. Julee and another volunteer immediately applied a charcoal poultice, and Adam felt relief right away. They continued the treatment, and he felt normal by the next day.

The only source of an unlimited water supply is the river, whose black water produces clean clothes. So, everyone carries soap and clothes down to the river, where they spend two hours washing everything by hand, soaping the clothes in the river and beating them on large rocks. Extra fun comes from visiting with friends, waving to people that float by in canoes, and enjoying a swim and/or a bath at the same time. "I've never had such an exquisitely decorated laundry room before, with colorful birds, monkeys, and crawly creatures to entertain us," Julee said, laughing.

At a staff meeting, Matthew pointed out that one lesson all volunteer missionaries must learn is to choose to fit their lives into God's plans. "God permits little irritating experiences in order to teach His children to be adaptable," he said. "If we give our complaints to Him, He will give us power to adapt cheerfully, even with a smile."

"You know how afraid I am of snakes and other crawling creatures," Julee offered. "But yesterday, God helped me not to scream when a huge lizard ran across the path in front of me."

Stephanie, a student missionary, added, "When I fill my cup for a drink, I try to thank God for the water while I wait for the dirt to settle. He even helps me remember not to drink too close to the dirt. I'm thankful for the pure water from the mountain. I'm so glad we don't have to drink that river water that turns dark from the vegetation growing along the river's edge."

Adam smiled. "I'm learning to thank God for the good exercise of hiking a mile up Rain Mountain to clear the leaves, crabs, dirt, or whatever else might be blocking the tubes that supply our entire campus with drinking water. Then when I come back starved, I try not to grumble when we have the same kind of soup for each meal, and often there are no second helpings."

Another girl said, "I'm remembering to cover the furniture and ask God to keep me from grumbling before I knock the termites down from the walls and ceiling in our room."

"What thrills me most is seeing the Holy Spirit working on our students," Matthew said thoughtfully. "More than half of our students are not Christians. Last Friday night when I presented the gospel message, I asked those who wanted to give their hearts to Jesus to stay after the meeting so we could pray together. Every student stayed! What a beautiful experience as we split into small groups. Each staff member began to teach the students the prayer of repentance and surrender."

Since God gives to each person a spiritual gift to use in blessing others, Matthew formed a leadership class to help students understand and discover the gift God had given to him or her. As they discovered their gifts, Matthew divided the students into groups to serve God in the nearby village of Paruima. The result was happy students working for God to bless others.

The Service Group cleaned an old lady's house and yard until they were immaculate. The Hospitality Group wrote cards of love and left flowers at various homes. The Encouagement and Prayer Groups visited and prayed with a lady dying from cancer. The Music Group sang to her. The Health Group made plans with the village leaders to start a free clinic for those hurting or in pain. The Preaching Group found five people with whom they will begin Bible studies. The Children's Group invited kids to come for a story time to tell them about Jesus. Enthusiasm pervaded the school as the Holy Spirit continued to give the students a vision of Jesus' life of service. Even the head cook reported, "I see the Holy Spirit working in the kitchen. Jesus multiplied the loaves and fishes for the five thousand. He's doing that for us, for lately I find we have leftovers after supper, when before we never had enough for all."

When the students went home for Christmas break, Matt and Julee spent a wonderful time with the student missionaries. Then by ham radio word came from Gary Roberts: "You will soon have a good problem. DIIC will be overstaffed. Another family, both physical therapists, will arrive in a few days, plus others who can fill your teaching and leadership duties. Would you be willing to expand God's work in other parts of Guyana? You could spend a few months in Kaikan, the village where David, Becky, and their family lived. There you could learn the Amerindian culture and do evangelistic work. Even though there's already a church in Kaikan, these people need the power of the Holy Spirit. I can't think of a better place to prepare for whatever God shows you. As you learn the Amerindian culture, you can branch out to surrounding villages."

Matt and Julee responded together, "We'll be glad to go wherever God leads and do what He wants us to do."

On Friday, January 7, 2005, Gary Roberts landed at Paruima's airstrip, loaded Matthew and Julee and their belongings, and took off for the fifteen-minute flight to the village of Kaikan, where the airstrip borders the little white church. The friendly people welcomed them with open arms and showered them with food and fresh fruit. Many people helped them carry their baggage as they walked the little trail that led to their new home.

The Guyana Conference had built a two-story wooden structure very near the river. Kitchen, visiting quarters, and a storeroom made up the first floor; upstairs were bedrooms and a balcony. Cooking was done on a one-burner kerosene stove. There was also a nice propane stove, but no propane. So, it remained unused. An outhouse and the lack of electricity and running water made this home like all the others in Kaikan. Since

Matthew and Julee's home near the river in the village of Kaikan. In the rainy season the river is prone to flooding—as Matthew and Julee discovered!

the rainy season had begun, the single solar panel did not receive enough sunlight to charge the battery that would give lights and limited power. Visits to the outhouse provided a kind of entertainment. Huge spiders crawled on the walls, and cockroaches scampered on the floor!

The villagers gave Matthew and Julee more bananas than they could eat. For Sabbath breakfast, Julee fried plantains (large bananas) and made a fruit salad of papaya, bananas, and fresh coconut milk. Trees near the house were loaded with coconuts. Cashew nuts from trees in their yard added a special touch. What a delicious breakfast!

At church on Sabbath the elder surprised them with the announcement, "This will be a special week of prayer. God has sent the pastor at the right time to teach us about the Holy Spirit. His wife will lead out in the Kids' Corner, as well as the music."

On Sunday they cleaned the kitchen, prepared for the evening meeting, and enjoyed the many visitors who came to get acquainted. The local people seemed very happy and contented. A local GAMAS worker, known to everyone as Uncle Claude, called from the door, "Come see something I found just a few feet away. I felt something touch my leg and looked down at one of the most poisonous snakes in Guyana, a two foot long labaria. I jumped back, grabbed a stick, and God helped me kill it immediately. I thank Him for my life!" And he held up the limp creature.

Matthew and Julee found it challenging to adjust to living like the villagers with all the bugs, mice, bats, and dirt. There were no glass windows. The floors had cracks between each board, so the outdoor creatures could come and go as they pleased. Worst of all, the fruit flies and ants got into everything. The pesky weevils quickly discovered the flour and other food they had brought from Georgetown. They tried to pick them out but dared not throw the food away because there was no more.

However, the peaceful living so close to nature also had great rewards. Matthew and Julee loved the visits of the hummingbirds. One large type of hummingbird came into the house all the time and built a nest in one of the rooms. The busy pair's visits seemed normal and delightful. Not quite so welcome were the "baboons" in the trees along the river who began to scream between three and four o'clock in the morning. Matthew and Julee thanked God for teaching them to enjoy the sound of the river—the noise of crickets, frogs, and various bird and insect calls. Compared to the noise and bustle of Georgetown, the quiet peace of the jungle was refreshing, and they praised God for their surroundings as they enjoyed watching the monkeys play in the trees.

For a week rain poured down almost nonstop; this was more than even the locals were used to. People warned Matthew and Julee one day that their house could flood in the night because it was located right by the river. They hardly slept that night. Often they got up and shined the flashlight on the river to see if it had overflowed its steep banks. At 4:00 A.M. the water was a foot from the top of the bank. At 5:00 A.M. it had risen another six inches. On the radio, they called Uncle Claude, who had lived in their house before. He came in the dark and looked at the river.

"There's nothing to worry about yet," he assured them. "Once the river starts overflowing its banks, it seeps slowly; so, there's plenty of time to move your stuff upstairs." They went back to bed and slept until 6:00 A.M. They awoke to find the river was slowly filling the yard. They moved everything upstairs just in case the water rose higher. "Once when the Gates lived in this house, the downstairs was flooded in four feet of water," the neighbors related. "They actually paddled their canoe into the house!"

About 11:00 A.M. the water was two inches from covering the floor. Then one inch. Then it stopped rising! The water level stayed there all day but started going down during the night. Though the rain continued, the river didn't flood again.

Matthew near the river home in Kaikan during the height of the flooding.

While Matthew and Julee were moving all their personal goods upstairs, a villager came running and shouted, "A man that was in church Sabbath just died. He's a prominent father in the village. Everyone knows him well. You'll find his house in the flooded area."

Quickly Matthew and Julee put on their boots and slipped and slid down the muddy trail. A group of people had gathered. Weeping women stood close by the dead man's bed. Matthew asked, "Could you please tell us what caused his death?"

The head elder of the church spoke with fear in his eyes. "*Kanima* [evil spirits] killed this man."

Shocked, Matthew listened as the church members confirmed their strong belief in spiritualism.

Julee asked about the man's symptoms. The family replied, "He has had pain in his left shoulder and tightness on the left side of his chest for several days. He also complained of being short of breath. But he ignored it. The morning he died, he said he felt better. Suddenly, he felt a numbness on his left side. He struggled for breath and soon died."

Julee spoke quietly, "Those are sure symptoms of a heart attack. Or it could have been a pulmonary embolism. Since you can't do autopsies in Kaikan, we will never know exactly, but likely a fatal heart attack caused his sudden death."

However, even the Christian Amerindians seemed to cling to the demonic beliefs that cause them to live in fear. Any sudden or unexplained death is credited to the *kanima.* They say these evil spirits travel with hunters. If he doesn't provide them with enough blood to drink, they turn on humans and kill them. Satan has been building a fortress of fear around these precious people for hundreds of years. These superstitions from the witch doctors are passed down from the elderly and accepted by the youth. What a challenge to bring the light of trust and faith to dispel the darkness! Only then will the people reject the power of the master deceiver and rely on God's great power to destroy these traditional beliefs. Matthew and Julee continually prayed for the outpouring of the Holy Spirit's power on the dear people of Kaikan.

The Amerindians work as subsistence farmers, relying heavily on cassava and the produce from their farms for food. Unfortunately, wild pigs came in large groups earlier that year and ate or destroyed most of their garden produce. This devastation affected many families. The villagers pressed together, sharing what they had and trusting God to provide. Matthew and Julee had saved a box of pasta for a treat. But, alas, weevils found their way in. They had no choice but to carefully pick them out and eat the pasta. As long as the food didn't make them sick, they rejoiced that they had something to eat.

San Juan, a small village across the river in Venezuela, needed a new church. So, the Kaikan members hiked for two hours to help. Construction in the interior of Guyana differs greatly from the way it is done in North America. First the builders hike through the jungle, sometimes for hours, looking for the right kind of trees. Then they fell the trees with chain saws, cut them into logs, and finally into boards. Heavy hardwood is cut into boards fourteen to twenty feet long and weighing from forty to seventy pounds each. That day spent hauling boards for the church construction meant a total of five-and-a-half hours of walking through the jungle. Each man, including Mat-

Bringing in the man who was bitten by a poisonous labaria snake. This snake is a deadly menace in the jungles of Guyana.

thew, carried one board to the church building site. Then they hiked back home to Kaikan.

Seldom does anyone venture out after dark in the jungle, but one early evening Matthew and Julee heard a knock on the door. Holding a twelve-inch, yellow-tailed labaria snake draped over his cutlass, the man exclaimed, "My wife has just been bitten." Camouflaged by a dark pattern, this poisonous snake is a deadly menace.

With prayers darting heavenward, Matthew and Julee gathered up charcoal and the snake-bite kit and ran to the victim's home. Julee immediately

Julee applied a charcoal poultice to the area of the snake bite— the foot and ankle—and gave the man a charcoal mixture to drink. Charcoal helps to neutralize the venom. And she prayed for God's healing as she continued to care for the victim.

got the battery-operated shocking machine ready, which neutralizes the venom. The bite was below the ankle on the inside of the woman's foot; so, Julee applied the shock from the knee down. Then she covered the injured foot and ankle with a charcoal poultice and gave the woman charcoal to drink. The woman didn't like the mixture and drank it slowly, even throwing a whole cup on the ground when she thought they weren't looking.

After a couple of hours she began coughing up blood. As Julee worked, she prayed desperately, "God, the venom injected into her body is getting into the blood stream. It's thinning her blood, causing internal bleeding. Her gums have also started to bleed, but her blood pressure remains good. Please help the charcoal to do its work."

She continued praying while she changed the charcoal poultices and urged the woman to keep drinking the charcoal drink. Gradually the victim began to relax. Free from pain at last, she sank into sleep and slept most of the night.

If a person can survive the first twenty-four hours after being bitten by a poisonous snake, they usually will survive. This woman lived. Matthew and Julee rejoiced that God had blessed their simple remedies and that He had saved this woman's life by His healing power.

The village of Arau, Guyana, where Matthew and Julee held evangelistic meetings. The people couldn't get enough of the messages!

God blessed the three months they spent in Kaikan. The last of March Matthew and Julee set out for the small village of Arau. Traveling by boat for two hours, they then hiked through the jungle for another six hours.

In Arau the people were eager to hear the gospel and see the pictures Matthew and Julee brought. They gladly helped set up a small borrowed generator, electrical wire, and a light bulb. With these, they began evangelistic meetings in the little white church. Julee used a battery-powered keyboard to teach them hymns and songs of praise. How they loved to sing!

A mother and child in the village of Arau. Many of the villagers were concerned about spirits and their influence on their daily lives.

Sabbath morning Matthew preached about superstition and spiritualism. The evening meeting began at 5:30 P.M., with a question-and-answer session about evil spirits, spells, and charms. One questioner wanted to know, "Is it good to call on the spirits of animals or some other natural object and blow on the sick for healing, as the witch doctors teach?" Another asked, "Is it bad to mingle our blood with the blood of reptiles so our hunting expeditions will be successful?" Such questions kept coming from these simple Seventh-day Adventist Christians, who, without someone to teach them the Scriptures, were unknowingly involved with Satan on a daily basis. The questions kept coming until 8:30 P.M.

Matthew began to close the meeting, but the people called out, "We want more song service. We'd like to see the pictures. Aren't you going to teach us?"

"You mean you want the entire meeting now—after we've already had three hours of discussion?"

"Yes, yes. We seldom have a minister. Please stay."

Thrilled at their desire to hear Bible truth, Matthew and Julee were rejuvenated even though the meeting lasted until 11:30 P.M. Evidence of the Holy Spirit came when one man gave his heart to Jesus and pledged to follow Him the rest of his life. How glad Matthew and Julee were to be called of God to serve these precious souls in isolated places.

Gary Roberts then flew them from Arau to a place called Eteringbang. Meanwhile, they felt impressed that the Holy Spirit was calling them to the forbidden village of Kurotoco. Inaccessible by plane or any other kind of vehicle, Kurotoco could be reached only by boat on a very dangerous river for twelve hours one way. Many miners have drowned on the unpredictable Cuyuni River.

Not only was it incredibly hard to get to, Kurotoco was a forbidden village. A few years earlier, GAMAS had sent Amerindian Bible workers to Kurotoco to start laying a foundation for a mission station. Each Amerindian village has a chief or head of the village. In Kurotoco the chief was an Anglican priest who did not want any Bible workers in his village. He ordered them, "You must leave within three days. I forbid you to return!"

Though this chief professed to be a priest, he did not know God nor practice His love. After Sunday church services he would invite the people to his home with the words, "The first drink is free," knowing their addiction would demand more. He sold these uneducated people alcohol and made them pay for all the free medications provided by the government.

Because it was difficult and expensive to travel to Kurotoco, government health officials seldom visited, so the village had no health care.

While in Kaikan, Matthew and Julee heard that the chief of Kurotoco might accept a medical team. They hired a government-employed dentist and offered their services. Since the village had received no medical care for the past two years and desperately needed help, the chief accepted their offer. So, they prayerfully prepared to enter this unknown, hostile world.

At Eteringbang, they hired an experienced boatman who charged them $320 for a round trip to Kurotoco. He furnished a twenty-one-foot dugout canoe, gasoline for the motor, and flat wooden seats for the trip. The medical/missionary team bought food supplies and extra fuel. The twelve-hour trip began. They snaked their way down the river, avoiding rapids and whirlpools. On the way they stopped when they saw people or their houses. Mining has polluted the Cuyuni River terribly. At one settlement of three families, they saw about twenty-five people, all of whom had a fever, caused by malaria, typhoid fever, cholera, or other diseases. Without medical treatment, if they live, they feel continually sick, never recovering from their illnesses. Most of them do not know how old they are or their last names. They exist in a sick, drunk, superstitious, fearful world.

As soon as the group entered Kurotoco, they set up a medical clinic. People came in a steady stream. The dentist pulled teeth while Julee treated those she could. Matthew had prayed all the way that he could establish a friendly relationship with the chief. As they visited, Matthew could see the priest softening. God seemed to convince the man that they sincerely wanted to help the village people.

"Chief, if you will open up an airstrip, our pilot can bring needed supplies, medicine, and even a teacher for your village children. You already have an empty school building. Wouldn't you enjoy seeing the little ones learn to read and write? If people become very sick, they can be taken to a doctor. If you wish, I could set up a ham radio for you now and show you how to make contacts."

The priest muttered, "That would be our first communication ever with the outside world." When Matthew made contact with Georgetown and heard a voice answer him, the priest smiled.

Matthew avoided the subject of religion, but he kept praying. Finally the priest said, "My people seem to have no hope and live in constant fear. Could you give them the simple gospel of belief and faith in God?"

Matthew smiled, "That would bring joy and hope to each one. God can change your village so that you would soon be the happiest people on the river."

Can God still work miracles on human hearts? Due to the influence of the Holy Spirit, this chief accepted the volunteer missionaries as friends, realizing they had not come to compete with him. Before they left, he pledged to open an airstrip and asked that they return. He even suggested that maybe they could bring a teacher to open a school for all ages and start a medical clinic.

God will surely finish what He started. He will change attitudes and make it possible for a little church to be built in Kurotoco where the people can worship the only God who can set them free from fear, alcohol, and sickness. God is well able to pour out His blessings and bring joy and hope to this forbidden village.

A Thousand Ways to Provide for Our Needs

From the volunteers in the jungles of Guyana to the television networks in Bolivia and Brazil, God continues to remind His volunteers that He is a God who works miracles to sustain His work. Just as the Brazil station went on the air, the remainder of the one-million-dollar purchase price came due. Another organization stood waiting, with cash in its pocket, wanting to buy the station. For David to be able to complete the sale and fund the operation of the station could happen only in answer to God for another miracle.

As David prayed for divine wisdom, He received a very strong impression from God: *"Take possession of the territory God has already given you in Bolivia. You have TV licenses for several cities where you haven't gone on the air. Refocus and complete the job begun in Bolivia."*

"But God, You know I have only enough money to pay for gasoline for the plane and other fees. How can I expand in Bolivia?"

"David, you will know what to do when you get there. Go in faith!"

Immediately after landing in Santa Cruz, Bolivia, David met with Remberto Parada, ADVenir's director, and Scott Grady, production manager. After sharing the conviction God had laid on his heart, David began outlining current opportunities and needs, remembering the promise "When we give ourselves wholly to God, and in our work follow His directions, He makes Himself responsible for its accomplishment" (Ellen G. White, *Christian Service*, p. 261).

The three men studied present needs. They compiled a challenging list:

1. Purchase small plots of land in three cities where broadcast licenses have previously been issued.

2. Put up transmitter stations and towers on these pieces of land.
3. Purchase new transmitters, antennas, and downlinks for each of the three cities.
4. Increase transmitter power and make antenna improvements in four other cities.
5. Meet equipment needs in the network studio.
6. Build a dormitory building for women in the prison. (The governor of the female prison had warned the Prison Ministry Group that they would lose the donated land within the prison walls unless they immediately began to build a desperately needed dormitory.)

All these projects totaled nearly $150,000—ten times normal monthly operating costs!

They looked at each other, and then Scott asked, "Are we to obey God's command to go to all the world even in the face of economic disaster?"

David answered this question with several additional questions: "Do we deny Christ the obedience He expects by depending on 'our' resources and 'our' abilities? If God's people don't stand up now and seize this opportunity, will God raise up others who will carry the Advent message to the world?"

Pastor Parada summarized the situation. "We are facing a financial dilemma, and it would be easy to point to a lack of resources to justify refusing to go forward. On the human side, going further into debt could mean failure and a loss of credibility, thus placing at risk the very work God has given us to do. Let's pray together for Scripture guidelines that will show us Gods' revealed will."

After they rose from their knees, they opened their Bibles. Scott read Matthew 25:14–30 and said, "The Master didn't expect His stewards to produce the money. He expected them to invest what He had given them. I'd say our first guideline is accountability—to God."

"And our second guideline, obviously, must be obedience to His expressed will," added Remberto Parada. "His command speaks plainly to us in Matthew chapter twenty-eight, verses eighteen to twenty, where He says that we are to go into all the world and preach the gospel."

"The third principle is the one Jesus gave to the rich young ruler in Matthew chapter nineteen, verses sixteen to thirty when He told him to sell everything he had and give to the poor so he could follow Him," David said. "And Matthew chapter ten, verse thirty-eight tells us that if we don't take up our cross and follow Him, we're not worthy of Him. That tells me that we must be willing to risk everything. And the fourth guideline, I believe, is that we should use what we have in our hands."

They sat in silence thinking. Then Scott reached for a book on a nearby shelf. He opened the book at a place he had already marked in the past. "Listen to this," he said. " 'Prompt and decisive action at the right time will gain glorious triumphs' [Ellen G. White, *Prophets and Kings*, p. 676]. To paraphrase this, we could say that opportunity determines timing. I think that is a fifth principle."

Pastor Parada spoke slowly and deliberately. "Presumption is Satan's counterfeit of faith. Both faith and presumption claim God's promises. Faith brings forth obedience, but presumption excuses transgression. Presumption leads us to involve ourselves in temptations that result from lack of prayer and meditation, plus violation of the laws of nature and prudence. In this situation we must be sure our decision is in harmony with clear Scripture teaching. We must avoid presumption and get our orders totally from God's Word."

"I have a special concern I'd like you to consider," David said. "As president of Gospel Ministries International, I am totally dependent upon God for everything. I feel embarrassed and even disrespectful to beg Him for more when I haven't used what He has already given me. Jesus said, ' "He who is faithful in what is least is faithful also in much" ' [Luke 16:10]. I realize that most business administrators feel they must continue to increase their financial reserves. But the Holy Spirit has convinced me that as we near the final events of earth's history, we should *reduce* our reserves and invest them all in God's work now while we have the opportunity. Could it be that the more reserves we corporately and individually store up for the future, the less God can trust us to finances during the crisis we face today? Could we add this principle to our list— don't ask for more until you use what you already have?"

Scott answered, "Jesus said in Luke chapter six, verse thirty-eight that as we give, more will be given to us. I've tried this personally, and I've learned that God loves to give us more when we give more. To put this in modern terms, we could say, Don't commercialize God's blessings."

"Right now it seems that God is asking us to do the impossible, to live outside our comfort zone. What is our part?" asked Pastor Parada.

"The vital lesson, I believe," David answered, "is total dependence on God. If I really believe Jesus is coming very soon, I'll show my belief by acting on what I believe."

Pastor Parada interrupted, "I must share with you what happened last night. The Lord woke me at two in the morning. In my thirty-one years of ministry, I've never had a more intense encounter with God. I could only tell Him that, by His power and grace, I would act with Him, follow His orders, and leave the results in His hands."

"Before we make our final decision, let me call to find out if any funds have become available before we make our next move," David said. He came back shortly to report that no new funds had become available.

After the three men prayed again, Pastor Parada spoke with conviction. "We have one thing in our favor: credibility with vendors and manufacturers with whom we have had dealings. Depending totally on God, I will place orders for seven more transmitters and the necessary equipment. We'll dispatch a man to purchase small plots for the TV transmitters and towers in three cities. We'll begin construction of the women's prison dormitory immediately. God has told us to visit those in prison, and we must go forward by faith to obey His revealed will. We must spread the gospel message. Let's trust that God will care for the entire amount of nearly one hundred fifty thousand dollars. I can imagine Jesus is saying to Gabriel, 'I'm filled with joy that some of My children on earth are willing to trust us completely and go forward.' "

A short time later David made a trip to the United States. A pastor friend called him the day after his arrival. "My wife and I heard about your recent commitments in Bolivia. We have decided to take out a mortgage on our home. The equity could be working for the Lord instead of just sitting there. If Gospel Ministries International will be responsible only for keeping up the loan payments, the mortgage money belongs to Him. Use it now."

This donation, together with other incoming funds, covered all the liabilities incurred up to that time. Far from losing credibility in South America, GMI rejoiced in the increased financial influence these purchases brought to the television network.

A short time later David learned more about how God does the impossible. David was flying with Gary Roberts and asked, "Gary, how have you managed to keep two planes in the air during these last six months with such a tight cash flow? Have you been receiving donations from outside sources?"

"No, I've had no additional cash except what you have sent me." Gary paused and then continued, "Strangely, each month I have enough funds in the account to pay my bills. Recently I took time to look closely at my statements. I realized that many of the checks I wrote haven't cleared for five months. They appear to have disappeared somewhere between Guyana and the United States. My balance in the U.S. remains unchanged!"

"Has the bank in Guyana complained because it hasn't received its money?"

"Never," Gary answered. "The account is in balance. Maybe I'll never know the mystery of the disappearing checks until I get to heaven. Meanwhile, the medical aviation program in Guyana is going forward at full speed."

"That reminds me of one of my favorite quotes," David said. " 'Our heavenly Father has a thousand ways to provide for us, of which we know nothing. Those who accept the one principle of making the service and honor of God supreme will find perplexities vanish, and a plain path before their feet' " (Ellen G. White, *The Desire of Ages*, p. 330).

Accomplished Only by God

The telephone rang, and David heard the caller say, "This is Robert Costa, Spanish language evangelist for *It Is Written*. Do you think you could squeeze Pastor Mark Finley into your next satellite evangelism campaign in Caracas?"

Knowing there is usually a four-year waiting list for Pastor Finley's appointments, David quickly answered, "I'm sure we could arrange that. Tell me more."

"After working with you in your February satellite campaign in Maracaibo, Venezuela, Dr. Milton Peverini and I returned to *It Is Written* and shared our excitement at seeing such a large secular audience being reached. Your strategy to air the series concurrently on several large commercial television networks encouraged Pastor Finley to donate his vacation time in order to make himself available for the Caracas campaign."

Immediately David began working with the union, conference, and university to coordinate the event with ADVenir. The eight-day series was carried around the world by three church satellite networks and four secular networks. Each night of the meeting, viewers responded through phone calls and e-mails, and these continued into the following day. One e-mail came from faraway Turkey!

Of course, the enemy tried to keep the signal off the air. The day before the meetings began, the company providing the satellite uplink advised David that they would not be able to provide the service as promised because the church is located in a politically sensitive area of town.

The company recommended using an uplink truck, but the price would be nearly twice the cost. God blessed the negotiations for an uplink truck and the final price was less than half of what was first asked. The meetings began on schedule.

Two days later, the governor of the state contracted with the company for a network uplink for his political campaign. Unfortunately, this disabled the signal on which ADVenir and 3ABN depended. Those handling the network for the meetings scrambled to set up a new dish in Bolivia that could pick up a different signal. They were able to get the new dish aligned just five minutes before the uplink for the meeting needed to begin! That same evening the uplink truck showed up late due to an accident on the freeway. The truck locked onto the satellite and got the signal on the air just seven minutes before the meeting began. Satan was trying hard to keep the meetings from being broadcast, but God won on a very tight schedule. The last three days of the meetings went smoothly.

Two services in the large El Paraiso Adventist Church were required each evening to handle the large number of those wanting to attend the meetings. One viewer called from the city of Punto Fijo in northern Venezuela to say that the meetings were causing a revolution in thinking among viewers in his neighborhood.

Two days after the meetings began, David flew to Puerto Ordaz, Venezuela. When he was returning, an immigration officer at the airport asked, "What is your destination?"

"Caracas."

"Are you working with the meetings by Pastor Finley that started two days ago?"

"Yes, but how did you know? I didn't know Puerto Ordaz had a local TV station or that cable companies carried ADVenir's signal here."

"Evidently the cable companies discovered the signal and decided to carry the meetings each night," the officer stated.

Only eternity will reveal how many persons watched Pastor Finley spread the gospel throughout Venezuela and much of the Hispanic world over ADVenir.

About this time Jenny Mendoza, who works full time with ADVenir and also is involved with the Bolivian prison ministry, received a call to come and pray for a sick prisoner at the Palmasola female prison in Santa Cruz, Bolivia. Jenny read promises from Scripture and knelt by the bed of the lady to pray. Halfway through her prayer, Jenny felt herself suddenly shaken by the shoulder and heard a voice say, "Get out right now!"

Turning around, she saw a Catholic nun who shouted, "You are a Protestant; you have no right to pray for a sick Catholic lady! Leave now!" And Jenny did.

A nearby prisoner asked the nun, "Do you know who that lady is that you just ran off?" The nun shook her head. "She works at the ADVenir station, the one we watch with you quite often."

"Oh!" exclaimed the nun as she went running after Jenny.

"Excuse me," she said, catching up to her. "I understand you work at ADVenir. Is that true?"

Jenny nodded, "Yes, I'm the program director for the network."

Smiling, the nun extended her hand. "Please forgive me for shouting at you like that. I would never have done that if I had known. You see, ADVenir is my favorite TV station. Would you come to my house for dinner tonight?"

Jenny happily accepted her invitation, and she still enjoys spending time with her new friend.

Everywhere David sees evidence of God working through ADVenir. At the ticket counter of the bus station in Santa Elena, Venezuela, he told the agent, "I'd like to buy a ticket for a friend," and he passed some money across the counter along with his friend's ID card.

The clerk was a nicely dressed young woman, wearing jewelry and bright red lipstick. She looked up. "I think I know this lady. Is she an Adventist teacher from Maracay?"

"Yes," David answered in surprise. "In fact she is our Union director of education. How did you come to know her?"

"I was an Adventist once. In fact I did colporteur work in Maracay when I knew her."

"Really? I wouldn't have suspected you of being an Adventist colporteur now. Did something happen?" Tears suddenly glistened in her eyes.

"Forgive me for crying. My name is Monica. I left the church years ago." More tears.

"Jesus loves you, Monica." David smiled in sympathy. "He wants you back working for Him."

"I would like that, but I can't," she sobbed. "It's impossible!"

"May I pray for you, Monica?" David asked. She nodded.

David slipped his hand through the small window opening, and she put her hand in his. "Lord, I pray for the restoration of Your will in Monica's life. Bring her back to a close relationship with You. Pour Your love upon her. In Jesus' name. Amen."

After the prayer, Monica explained, "Before I accepted work here, I made it clear I would not work on Saturdays, even though I haven't attended church for a long time. However, I recently decided that the next Sabbath I will be in church. You see, a short time ago I was at home on Sabbath. I turned on the cable network to watch Animal Planet. As I switched through the channels, I found a new station with a nature program that caught my attention. Fascinated by this new station, I kept watching. Later that evening I watched a sermon and recognized the Seventh-day Adventist message. I cried and cried as I watched. For several weeks now I've watched that station all day Sabbath and cried the whole time. I can' t resist any longer. This week I'm going back to church."

David pulled out his business card and slipped it across the counter.

"You're the president of ADVenir?" She began crying again. "That's the network I have been watching."

Later David returned to visit Monica and discovered her husband had abandoned her and her three small children. What a joy to encourage her!

One country! One small jungle town. One small cable network. One single person who longed to come back to Jesus. What joy all this causes in heaven! Certainly the angels keep busy visiting the five hundred thousand homes just in Venezuela that receive ADVenir by cable, not to mention viewers in Bolivia and Brazil. All the heavenly behind-the-scenes activity will be revealed in eternity. God cares about each individual and works miracles to bring them to Him.

God's message reaches even little children. In the fall of 2004 at the Adventist-Layman's Services and Industries (ASI) meetings in Cincinnati, Ohio, David shared the blessings and challenges of God's work in South America. He noticed a twelve-year-old girl sitting near the front of the auditorium. She seemed fascinated at the exciting stories he told of God's care and protection of the volunteer missionaries. A smile covered her face when he said, "You don't have to visit a foreign country or wait until you are grown up to be a missionary. You don't have to be a pilot, a teacher, or know how to operate a television network. You can be a volunteer missionary right where you are. But God does require that you love Him with all your heart and that you recognize that everything you have belongs to Him. You can learn more about the way God uses volunteers by watching our DVD. It contains four videos directly from the front lines. Just come to my booth and ask for one."

After the meeting, this girl—twelve-year-old Sarah—spent some time thinking about what David had said. *If all I have belongs to God,* she asked herself, *then why are my savings sitting in the bank? It isn't doing any good for God there.*

That evening, after the meeting, she got permission from her parents to go to the Gospel Ministries International booth where David and his team worked. She saw David talking to some people, so she waited until he was done. Then she got his attention by tugging on his sleeve.

"I'm Sarah," she told him, "and I have something to tell you." He bent down to listen. "I've decided that if God owns everything I have, then I must give it to Him to use. I have been saving my money for about five years. I have three hundred dollars. I want to give you all of it to use for God's work in the mission field."

"Oh, Sarah, that is so beautiful," David bent down to give her a hug. "I know God will be so happy with your gift."

"But I have a problem," interrupted Sarah. "You see, I'm not old enough to write a check. If I send cash in the mail, it might be lost. What should I do?"

Tears choked his voice as David hugged her again. "Don't worry, Sarah, your parents will help you to send it. Just remember, God will use your gift in a very great way to reach lots of people. Whenever you can, show people this DVD."

David was right. When Sarah's family and home church heard about her gift, they more than matched the amount Sarah had saved. Sarah spent the rest of that evening at ASI distributing hundreds of GMI's videos and sermon tapes to anyone she could find throughout the convention hall. Anyone who saw Sarah could see that her face was shining with joy.

One very wealthy man, after hearing Sarah tell what God was doing, accepted the tapes and DVD. He immediately visited GMI's booth. "I've come to confirm the miracle stories a little girl named Sarah told me. I've never seen a girl so enthusiastic and mission driven as that little girl. I just had to come and find out for myself if God really did give you one and a half million dollars for a network in Bolivia."

Sarah Shank and David Gates. As He did with the widow's mite in the New Testament, God used the sacrificial gift and missionary spirit of twelve-year-old Sarah to bring about far greater blessings than she ever imagined.

David enjoyed telling him of God's miraculous provision for Bolivia—and Brazil, as well. Then he told him the story of Sarah giving all her savings to God.

"That's amazing! What an unusual child!" the man exclaimed.

"Go thou and do likewise," David replied. The man walked away very quiet and sober.

Will Sarah's sacrificial gift and missionary spirit be as far reaching as the widow's mite? Only eternity will tell, but God did fulfill her dream to be a foreign missionary. She and her parents have accepted a call for overseas mission service.

But that isn't the end of the story. A few weeks after the ASI meetings, David sent an email telling about Sarah's gift. One reader was so touched by the story that she sent a gift for ten thousand dollars.

In Bolivia, God continued to care for the prison ministry. A twenty-five-thousand-dollar dormitory and work center for men was completed inside the men's prison in Santa Cruz. This building can accommodate forty-two men. The women's prison received fifteen thousand dollars to complete the construction of the women's dormitory. Now children could live with their mothers and not sleep out in the courtyard. The children's ministry group in the women's prison organized the older kids into a Pathfinder club—the first Pathfinder club organized and conducted in a prison!

In the jungle villages of Venezuela, Bob Norton continued his mission work. On one occasion he flew into the village of Apauri, a village on the edge of the savanna with a big mountain towering over it. He went to pick up a pastor whom he'd flown into the village a few days previously. When he landed, the pastor told him, "We have a big problem. A man in the church is extremely ill; it seems to be the same sickness his brother died from a few months ago. Also, of the two hundred cows they had, only eighty are alive. The others have died one by one. The Adventist church elders and deacons believe the chief of the village has cursed them and is responsible for these deaths and illnesses. They are even looking for ways to kill the village chief."

Bob and Neiba Norton's home in Venezuela. The Nortons face many challenges in their ministry to the people, but God continues to work miracles in their behalf.

Bob Norton flew the pastor to his home and took the sick man to a hospital, where the doctors tried to find out the cause of his illness. Meanwhile Bob returned to the village. The chief denied cursing the sick man or anyone else. He was afraid for his life. By this time, the fear and unrest had spread to a nearby village, as well. Bob called for a meeting of the two villages. He begged the people to live in peace and assured them that God is stronger than the devil. The Adventist church members agreed to fast and pray three times a day for two weeks for faith to believe in God and not fear the evil spirits.

Meanwhile everyone was waiting to see what would happen to the sick man in the hospital. Several others in the village had developed similar symptoms. Bob flew a team of doctors to the village so they could try to figure out what caused the death of the cattle and the sickness of the people. Meanwhile, faithful pastors and members joined with Bob praying that God, the great Healer, would heal the sick man. More importantly, they prayed for peace between the villages that were fighting, that the people would trust God and turn from their Satanic superstitious beliefs.

The sick man became unable to walk, and a doctor successfully operated on his upper legs. However, he came very close to death—not from the problem with his legs, which was not life threatening, but from his belief that he had been cursed and would die. Eventually, he returned home, and peace was restored between the villagers. Oh how these people need to understand better God's love and His ability to free them from Satan's power.

Besides emergency flights, Bob Norton kept busy transporting lay workers. Workers can go to villages in an hour by plane that used to take them days, even weeks, to reach on foot. Instead of visiting a village only every two years, Bible workers can now go out by plane for a month or more at a time to teach God's Word and then return home for a few days, get supplies, and leave again. Several new airstrips have been cleared in different villages.

Using just a machete, axe, shovels, and much muscle power and sweat, the people clear the land and prepare an airstrip where the mission plane can land. How do they get it level? They don't. They cut down the trees, dig out the stumps, and smooth the really big bumps—that's it! This strip of ground is now a runway. Bob tells them to make the strip at least a thousand meters long, but four hundred meters is about the average—not a safe length in jungle terrain.

Often Bob flies in fuel for outboard engines. Since many villages are located beside rivers, dugout canoes can navigate to dozens of other villages where no runways exist. Thus, more people can be reached with the gospel through this means of travel.

The good news is that Bob, Neiba, and their son, Josiah, have moved into the house that they have been building for almost three years. No, it's not their home. Someday other families will come to the base and carry on the aviation program. But for now it provides a living place for them and for guests who come to help with the never-ending projects. No, it isn't finished, but that must wait till more money comes in. The windows do have glass and screens to keep out the bugs. The bathroom needs to have the plumbing finished, but the Nortons rejoice to be in a place they can call home and that is large enough to share with others.

Besides the fuel shortages and long waiting lines, Bob faces another serious problem. His work is hampered by the limitations of the small Cessna 172. Short, rough airstrips mean he often can take only one passenger at a time, leaving many waiting. Often he lands and takes one person and part of their things to a longer airstrip. He leaves them there and returns to get another person, weighing everything carefully that must be transported. When he reaches the maximum weight for a safe takeoff, he must leave the rest. Then he prays that the weather will be good so that he can get to home base with everyone while there is still daylight in which to fly. Often while in flight, he will get an emergency call on the radio, such as the time a little girl was bitten by a poisonous snake. When that happens, pastors or Bible workers who are waiting for Bob to take them somewhere may have to stay where they are another day or so. But Bob will come and get them as soon as possible.

Bob needs a larger, safer, more powerful airplane. He puts his life on the line every time he lands to save a life. He prays constantly, knowing that landings and takeoffs on these extremely short, rough strips are not really safe. He is depending on God to impress others to help in the purchase of a larger plane. He knows that God will provide, that He has children who will share what He has given them to make this life-saving work more fruitful.

CHAPTER 19

Loss or Gain Is in God's Hands

Shortly after God opened an opportunity for Gospel Ministries International to purchase—on faith—a million-dollar TV station in Brazil, David was scheduled to speak at an ASI convention held at Cohutta Springs, Georgia. After one of the meetings a young couple stopped by to speak with him.

"My name is Daniel Spencer," began the young man. "I am from Portugal, and my wife, Sarah, is from Brazil. We were so touched by your message tonight. God has been impressing us for some time to work for Him. Do you have a place we might serve?"

"Praise the Lord!" exclaimed David, his heart filling with joy. "I believe you are the answer to my prayer for a director for our new station in Brazil. Let's pray together that God will direct every step of the way."

David was greatly encouraged by this evidence of divine intervention. God had provided the down payment of $150,000 for the Brazil station, plus another $50,000 a short time later. Now He had provided an energetic, dedicated director who spoke Portuguese. Remembering God's powerful hand providing for Bolivia, David wondered how God would resolve the matter of the $800,000 balance due in four months to complete payment for the Brazil station. As agreed, the sellers relocated the transmitter site to a new building and tower that provided better coverage for the giant city.

The deadline for paying the remainder of the purchase price occurred while David was in the United States. As the day drew closer, David received several phone calls from Brazil to remind him that the account was due. Knowing God will never fail those who put their trust in Him,

David assured the staff that God had a plan. Twenty-four hours before the funds needed to be paid, David received a phone call from a friend

who said, "We're selling our family business. When the sale is complete, we will have between eight hundred thousand and nine hundred thousand dollars to donate to your broadcasting work!"

David immediately called the sellers in Brazil with the good news. Though the funds would not be available until the donor's company was sold, God had al-

Daniel and Sarah Spencer and their children. When Daniel, who speaks Portuguese, became the director for the new TV station in Brazil, it was an answer to prayer.

ready providentially provided two payments on the exact dates the sellers set. Now David awaited God's timing on the remainder.

In Brazil, even many very poor people have a satellite dish on their roofs. An engineer told David, "More than fourteen million dishes point to B-one Brazilsat. It is the most popular Brazilian satellite, and it is growing by fifty to seventy thousand users across the country each month. If you could get on the B-one satellite, you could reach almost the entire country of Brazil with just one station. But it is impossible to find any space on that satellite; all the space has been filled for years. No one can buy space at any price."

David smiled, "God enjoys doing the impossible. When He wants a job done, He makes the space available in His own time. When God gives an order to go into all the world, He opens the way as we obey Him."

David's friend shook his head in disbelief but promised, "I'll make contacts with B-one satellite for you. Just remember, I have no hope there will ever be any more space."

A few months later, Daniel Spencer informed David that the rented three-story studio and office building was ready for the inauguration ceremony. So, Pastor Remberto Parada, ADVenir director in Bolivia who speaks fluent Portuguese, flew with David to Brazil. Many enthusiastic young professionals, representatives from the different Adventist churches in the city, came and offered their talents to serve the Lord. Even the sellers of the station were present.

One of the key men controlling satellite space for three of Brazil's largest networks came and decided to stay for the service. He wanted to see firsthand what type of programming the station offered. He became enthusiastic as he learned of God's leading. "I feel privileged," he said, "to be invited to be a part of this great project for Brazil. I'm here to discuss uplink possibilities on one of Brazilsat's satellites. I promise to use all my influence to ensure the signal will get national visibility on Brazil's best satellite."

God's people in Brazil are witnessing an answer to many years of prayers. They rejoice with courage to see what God is doing for their country.

Month after month rolled by. Still the individual who had promised to send money for the Brazilian network was unable to do so because his business had not sold. The station in Brazil stayed on the air, but the sellers were facing a financial crisis. The first half million dollars had been paid on time. Believing the remaining funds would soon be forthcoming, the sellers decided to take out a loan from the bank to cover their needs and repay it when the remainder of the funds were paid. Months rolled by, and near the end of 2004 the sellers' bank demanded a settlement. At the same time, a Venezuelan cable company had completed installing ADVenir's signal nationwide and was asking for immediate payment.

With a heavy heart, David turned to his wife, Becky. "We're beginning a new year with a lot of unsolved problems. Sometimes I'm tempted to despair. But I know God has led us before."

"God has a plan," she encouraged David. "I'm sure of it. We just have to trust Him."

But as day followed day with no answer from God, the temptation to worry increased. Then just when they needed something to bolster their faith, David and Becky received a lengthy e-mail from longtime missionary friends. Its contents touched their hearts and filled them with renewed courage and trust in God. In part, this is what they read:

Dear David and Becky,

I appreciate that you have been praying for us. God's soldiers have to be stronger than regular ones. We come to the battlefield, but not alone—we bring our entire families.

Not all of God's blessings come in times of prosperity. Some blessings come in a tribulation time. Most of my "soldiers" have deserted, my "fort" is taken, and my resources are running low. But the "soldiers" that are still with me are producing; and I've been learning and growing spiritually. I know that like Joseph in Egypt, many times the way down is the way to success. If we trust our lives to the Lord, we must also trust His managing, and know He is able and in control. What if Joseph had given up in the hard part of the process? He would never have become the prime minister and saved his family and people. The Lord is preparing us for something really big, and that requires hard training.

I firmly believe testing and difficulties are part of the preparation, and those who prevail until the end will see the prize that awaits us ahead. Like Job, we must learn to trust God in the bad moments when everything seems to fail, so that we shall not be proud and self-confident when the tremendous blessings come.

I won't lie to you—these are difficult moments. But where trouble abounds, grace and miracles superabound. We've seen the hand of the Lord, and have felt His touch almost literally.

I know the Lord can do anything whenever He chooses. My concern is that we may not fail in doing our part. If we fear now, if we faint at this very light testing, how will we survive in the future? We were told that this is what it would be all about in the final days. Here we are; the time has come, and we are part of the prophecies now.

Your companions,
The Spencers

This ringing declaration of trust in God's leading brought new courage to David and Becky as they pondered the future.

David pointed to his briefcase and said to Becky, "I'm holding proposed projects worth nearly thirty million dollars in that briefcase. These projects will reach throughout the entire country of Brazil. That doesn't include programs for additional expansion in other Latin American countries. Or the new television network for Romania with a one-point-four-million-dollar satellite contract already signed. Basically, all of these projects are humanly impossible. But how could I say no to these opportunities after all that God has done for us in the past?"

Becky's faith reached out to meet the challenge. "The very fact that all this is impossible in our own strength seems to me to be the strongest argument that God expects us to do it by His power and in His time. God will do greater and greater things as we come closer to the end."

"I know that's true," David nodded, "but I keep wrestling with a question one of our devoted volunteers raised. He asked me, 'David, how can we continue accepting new projects when our current ones struggle so much?' I'm not sure what God's answer would be. I've read what Ellen White wrote in the book *Evangelism*. It's right on this point." He opened the book lying nearby and read from pages 79 and 80:

> We are in danger of spreading over more territory and starting more enterprises than we can possibly attend to properly, and they will become a wearing burden in absorbing means. . . .
>
> . . . Let not the means at your disposal be spent in so many places that nothing satisfactory is accomplished anywhere. It is possible for the workers to spread their efforts over so much territory that nothing will be properly done in the very places where, by the Lord's direction, the work should be strengthened and perfected.

"At the same time, it sounds as though God wants balance, for on page eighty she also wrote, 'Keep up and increase the interest already started, until the cloud moves, then follow it.' Our problem seems to be that the cloud keeps moving at a rapid pace! The goal of every project we have is to bring people to Jesus. By God's grace, every project keeps growing. True, each one has its own problems, including an uncomfortable financial position. Each project depends on God from day to day. But has it ever been different? Even if we never adopted new projects, would it ever be easy?"

"No, I don't think it would," Becky answered quickly. "God plans what is best in His own timing. He knows us, and He keeps us humble and dependant on Him. He alone is able to provide and impress willing Christians to sacrifice and give. But He gives everyone free choice to obey or not. He's promised to supply all our needs according to His riches in glory by Jesus Christ" (see Philippians 4:19).

David gave Becky a hug. "You're such an encouragement to me. We must never get accustomed to God's miracles. I guess God wants us outside our comfort zone so we can continue to grow. The survival or loss of the Venezuela and Brazil networks will be determined very soon. Millions of souls are at stake. Our family, ministry partners, and volunteers have been praying for months. I know God can and will answer those prayers. For the last three days, God has woke me up with a praise song running through my mind. I'm waiting to see what He will do."

David and Becky knelt together to pray. "Thank You, Lord, for giving us another opportunity to trust You. Thank You for what You have done in the past to show that You are more than able to provide. We know You will do it again. For the sake of Your people who need to wake up and work as never before, for the sake of those dying in darkness around the world without knowing You, we pray that we will not fail to glorify Your name. Give us patience and faith to move only as fast as You want us to move. We know that when You want us to move, You will break the financial obstacles that currently block our way. We trust You; we love You; and we thank You, precious Lord. In Jesus' name, Amen."

CHAPTER 20

God's Love Builds Roads

After a short home leave, Jeff and Fawna Sutton arrived in the large city of Santa Cruz, Bolivia, in early February 2005. Their purpose? To buy a sturdy truck they could use for the many needs of operating a jungle school and farm—hauling construction materials, farm produce, brick, sand, gravel, wood, garden fertilizer, and people. They had received donations to buy a vehicle for the Richard Gates Technical Industrial School in Guayaramerin, in northern Bolivia.

The price of used trucks was quite high; so, they continually reminded God, "You know our limits, our great needs and the horrible roads. Please lead us to find a used truck that will last, be affordable. We know that's a big request, but You are a great God."

They searched Santa Cruz for a week. God helped them find a Nissan Condor they could afford. A trusted mechanic assured them, "This is a good truck. It may look large now, but it will perform well in rough terrain where you will need to use it."

Early Sunday morning Jeff and Fawna, along with Jeff's brother, Jason, and sister-in-law, Cheryl, and

Jeff and Fawna Sutton at the Richard Gates Technical Industrial School in Guayaramerin, Bolivia.

their two daughters, piled into the truck. Jason had come to help with school construction and airplane maintenance. Two other volunteers, Justin and Curtis, were on the trip, as well; they had arrived to work on school-building projects. The group of eight, plus all their baggage and supplies, began the long trip. They took turns driving night and day.

The truck, a Nissan Condor, that Jeff and Fawna purchased for the school in Guayaramerin, Bolivia.

They spread a tarp across part of the back of the truck. This, along with good sunscreen lotion, kept them from being fried by the sun, even though it was hot riding under the tarp. At night, the temperature cooled down. The last night they traveled on bumpy, dirt roads in the rain and got little sleep. They drank lots of water and praised God in song as they drove. After traveling forty-nine hours, they were extremely tired, so they stayed overnight in Guayaramerin, not far from the school. They thanked God for a safe trip and a good truck. God impressed someone to give them two Husqvarna brush saws to help keep the farm cleared.

The truck couldn't be driven directly the last distance to the school because of the condition of the road—more than a kilometer of gooey mud and water holes. Every time they tried, they got stuck. Getting the truck unstuck became a part of life. Get out the bottle jack, put wood under the sunken part of the truck, raise the truck and get out of the hole, then go a few hundred meters only to get stuck again. Each repetition of this process took from one to two hours. So, they decided either to walk in or drive the jeep.

Clearly, if the school was to grow, there must be a good road. Jeff asked a company to come and make an estimate of the cost of building a solid road. The man from the company offered to write a cheaper contract to help the school, but Jeff wondered if the final result would be adequate.

School opened with eighteen students. This was the second year of operation; so, there were freshman and sophomore classes, and the staff was hoping for an enrollment of thirty students. However, the school had only one classroom. Another was badly needed.

Early in March, Gary and Wendy Roberts, who direct the aviation work in Guyana, brought the Cessna 150, the very first plane David used in Guyana, for Jeff to fly. Gary and Jeff enjoyed a couple of days of flying together, testing some of the runways.

Unfortunately, with all his responsibilities at the school, Jeff had little time to fly. He was codirector of the school, in charge of keeping everything running smoothly. He handled the bigger discipline issues, made sure the staff was happy, and paid the stipends. Jeff valued his assistant, a very capable Bolivian, Enrique Sabala. Because Enrique understood the Bolivian culture, he was invaluable in handling discipline issues, buying food, and directing the farm. He was in charge of the students who worked in the industries: farming, carpentry, raising chickens, and a bakery. Enrique's wife, Sandra, an excellent cook, provided the food service. Short-term volunteers also came to help for different lengths of time. Jeff hoped that delegating responsibilities would free him for his medical aviation work, which is his great love.

In spite of her limited ability to speak Spanish, Fawna taught a health class to the students. As the school nurse, she also worked once a week in a clinic in the small town of El Yata, five kilometers away. This improved relationships with the community. She gave vaccinations, did prenatal checkups for the pregnant women in the community, and taught midwifery classes.

In March the happy couple moved into their little house. The floor, roof, and walls in their bedroom were completed. There wasn't enough lumber to complete the rest of the house, but Jeff and Fawna were thrilled to have their own home, even if it was only one room and a big porch with a roof over it.

With the help of short-term volunteers, they started to clear the land to build a concrete house for the volunteers who come and go. With their personal funds, Jeff and Fawna bought a motorcycle, so they could travel to town to do school business.

Even though the calendar said April, the road wasn't started yet. They had been waiting weeks for the low spots in the existing road, which were full of water, to dry out. During this time God continually sent His angels to guard their truck, which they had to park by the main road. In poor countries like Bolivia, batteries, tires, diesel, etc. disappear quickly. But nothing was stolen from their truck during all this time.

Finally the director of the road building company sent a tractor driver to see if the road was dry enough to work. "How long have you been doing this work?" Jeff asked the driver.

"Eighteen years."

"How long has the director been with the company?"

"Two months."

Jeff realized suddenly that the tractor drivers, not the director, were really in charge of the job. "What do I need to do to get the project started?" he asked the driver.

"Don't worry," the man replied. "I'll talk to the director. I can bring the tractor out tonight, and we can begin tomorrow morning."

As work on the road began, the staff prayed each morning in their worship that the Lord would keep rain off the road. In the tropics, mornings are usually clear, but heavy thunder storms come each afternoon. Jeff told the truck drivers who were hauling gravel, "If God can protect our truck for two months, He can keep the road dry."

But the very next day it began to sprinkle! "God, if it rains hard," Jeff prayed, "the crew will take away their equipment and never finish. Please send a miracle."

He could hear the sound of heavy rain a little distance away. Jeff had to make a trip on the motorcycle to the gravel pit. After he had covered about two hundred feet, rain began to fall so hard it hurt. For seven kilometers it poured. But when he arrived at the gravel pit, the rain had stopped and everything was dry! The men loaded their trucks. What a message God preached to these dump-truck drivers! Now they knew that the school staff served a living, loving God. God must have smiled as He gave them miracle after miracle.

And God had still another message to give the road crew. Almost all businesses in that part of the world operate by cheating, devising corrupt deals, and demanding bribes. God wanted these workers to learn a big lesson—that honesty and truthfulness bring blessings. The contract specified that the road to be built was to measure eight hundred meters in length. When Jeff took out his GPS and measured the road, to his surprise it measured seventeen hundred meters—more than twice as long as the contract indicated. Should he tell the contractors how long the road really was? Or should he fudge the truth? Could he lie and continue to be under God's blessing?

Jeff explained the mistake and told them that the road was actually twice as long as they had thought. The crew answered, "No problem. We can make the road that long, but we can't possibly finish before your Sabbath. And you've told us we can't work on your Sabbath. We can't let our equipment sit idle over the weekend. If you will let us work on Saturday, we can finish your road."

What to do? Jeff knew that if the crew left on Friday with the road not finished, they would never come back to complete it. Later that day the company director came back to check on the work. As she walked with Jeff along the road she asked, "You look sad. What's wrong?"

"Sometimes it's hard to be true and honest when it seems like suicide," Jeff replied. "But I know the only way this school will survive is through the blessings of God. You may think I'm crazy for not letting the crew work on Saturday, but I have no other choice but to honor and obey the God I serve." He explained the dilemma about working on the Sabbath.

After a few moments she spoke, "I think I can help you. I'll get the workers to switch their day off from Sunday to Saturday. It makes no difference to them. I'll get busy and extend the contract without stopping the work on the road."

"Thank you so much," Jeff smiled. "I knew God would help you work it out."

When they completed the road, the total cost was thirty-five hundred dollars. Jeff had enough to pay for the first contract, and half of the additional cost. With all the miracles God had done, the entire staff at the school eagerly waited to see what miracle their living God would do next. Jeff rejoiced that even though Satan was there to tempt him, God gave him the grace to live out before these people the principles of truth, obedience, and loyalty to a loving God. And God's love includes building roads!

Another of God's "mission miracles"—the new road leading to the Richard Gates Technical Industrial School.

In June a group arrived at the school to help build a house and to conduct evangelistic meetings in the village of El Yata. Besides Fawna's work in the clinic, the students led out each Sabbath afternoon in a youth meeting at El Yata. The local people loved the singing, Bible memorization, stories, and Bible trivia. These contacts helped make many friends, which they hoped to interest in Bible studies preparatory to the meetings. Several non-Adventist students from El Yata attend the Adventist school, and they opened their homes when rain poured down. Usually the meetings were held outside, and much of the village joined in.

God blessed the school with willing hands. New volunteers, who later became staff members, included two brothers from Oregon—one, a mechanic and the other, a gardener—who filled gaps the staff had neither time nor the skills to do. Another young lady arrived in time to teach.

Yes, God impresses young, skilled volunteers to take up pioneer work when the need arises—just as He used dedicated youth when the Adventist Church began. These young people have accepted God's call to service just as James and Ellen White did in the 1800s.

Not all volunteers are young people. Dr. Sheila Robertson, a retired physician in her midseventies, arrived in Guyana with the request,

"Please take me to the most isolated village where I can serve God and His people." In forty-five minutes David Gates flew her from Kaikan to Philippi, a village that would take five to six days to reach by foot through rugged jungle.

"Here's a little radio," David told her. "Please keep in touch every day, more often if you need to. Let us know what supplies you need." One day when David flew to Philippi for a short visit, Dr. Sheila exclaimed, "I love every minute sharing God's love with these wonderful people! Could I start a training school for Bible work-

Dr. Sheila Robertson hugs a villager in Paruima, Guyana. Dr. Robertson, a retired physician, asked to serve in an isolated area where she could accomplish the most good.

ers for adults and older youth? They have a big advantage; they speak the local dialects, and since they are Amerindians, they don't need government permission to visit other villages."

Dr. Sheila with a group of villagers beside the mission plane in the village of Philippi, Guyana. In a matter of minutes, the plane is able to take workers to remote villages like Philippi—a trip that would require five or six days on foot.

"Amazing! I've been thinking of starting the same kind of training school at Paruima," David said, "but I have no one to direct the program. Would you be willing to begin such a school there?"

"I like working in remote, isolated places best. Paruima is a large village of over six hundred. But if God needs me to head up a training school there, I won't say no." God surely worked through Dr. Sheila. As a result, for years many Amerindians have left the Bible worker training school and have gone to surrounding villages well equipped to give the gospel message to their people.

Now, Dr. Sheila has chosen to again serve as a pioneer missionary in the village of Lethem, which is strongly Catholic and Pentecostal. The little Seventh-day Adventist Church in Lethem isn't complete. The youth and small children meet in a lean-to, sitting on a pile of lumber. During June 2005, Dr. Sheila gave more than fifteen Bible studies a week. Since most people in Guyana speak and read English, she copied study materials for each of these persons so they could study on their own. Unfortunately, her computer and printer refused to cooperate and there was no one to fix them. So, she printed the Bible lessons by hand and then made copies on a photocopier. This dear volunteer, now in her eighties, loves to walk throughout the village giving out Bibles, books, and other literature. She says, "Rain or shine, bugs, insects, and mosquitoes—I don't worry about them. There's too much to do for Jesus, my constant Companion. I want to spend the time I have left sharing His love with others."

Chapter 21

The Airplane Crashes

"We need another school to train local missionaries," Gary Roberts announced to the GAMAS staff in January 2005. "More than half the students at Kimbia Mission Academy want to be involved in mission service. Other young people at DIIC and around Guyana also want to be trained to be missionaries. Let's begin a school in Bethany that will focus on evangelism, Bible work, nutrition, basic health care, and natural remedies."

"Melissa and I would be very interested in this," Gilbert Sissons responded enthusiastically. "We'd like to lead out in this new project. We could also start a wellness center in the future that would provide medical healing for people all around Guyana. That would give the students clinical experience too."

"Wonderful! Let's present the idea of starting a mission school to the Bethany village council. If the village leaders seem willing, we can begin construction of the buildings soon. I know we would have many students. Wouldn't it be great to begin by September 2006?" Gary was excited about the possibilities.

The Bethany village council voted unanimously in favor of the mission school project but wanted to present the idea to the community, as well. About 150 people came to a meeting to hear details about the mission project. They listened in silence. No one asked questions. Then someone spoke up. "We're convinced this project comes from God. We have only one question: When will the school open for students? We're all in favor of this project moving forward as soon as possible."

Later, the head elder of the Bethany Seventh-day Adventist Church told Gilbert, "This is a definite answer to my prayers. In fact, I sent to the United States for information about how to get training in Bible work and basic health care. I'm so thankful I won't have to leave Guyana to get this kind of education, that there is going to be a school right in my own village!"

Another lady said, ""I've been praying that God would provide something for the young people to help them stay in the church and do something worthwhile. What a God we serve!"

About this time God put a burden on the hearts of Christians in California to provide a boat for Guyana—to carry construction supplies and transport students and volunteer missionaries on the rivers of the interior of Guyana. Mel Brass, a member of the Adventist church in Ukiah, California, wrote, "We know you could use a boat in Guyana. We've found a sturdy fishing boat. Now we're refurbishing it and raising the funds to ship it to Guyana." The boat was shipped in August 2005.

God works miracles on the hearts of his faithful people to support His work.

There was room to build an airstrip at the site chosen for the Bethany school. Gary and Wendy longed to see an airplane hangar built there, as well. In July 2005, Gilbert Sissons began work at Bethany; the first project was a staff home. Melissa arrived in Bethany several weeks later with their two small children, Abigail, two, and her new little brother, Joshua, who was just a few months old.

A dental group from Romania planned to begin the health work by visiting most of the villages in the area. The next group of volunteers would arrive in November to begin work on the main school building/ wellness center. God blessed the project as the faithful group of workers moved forward.

Gary Roberts continued to face the problem of being the only pilot for two airplanes. There was an overload of needs, as well. He heard of Jim Craik, an experienced pilot from Troy, Montana, who, together with his wife, Lorraine, had responded to an invitation for volunteer mission work. Immediately Gary contacted Jim and Lorraine. "Please come and check out the joys and challenges of living, working, and flying in Guyana," he urged.

The day after Jim and Lorraine arrived in Guyana, Gary began introducing Jim to the unique airstrips in the country—everything from asphalt, long and short grass, and bumpy clay. Some approaches were good, others fair, and some far from desirable. But always the pilots received a welcome from the villagers as they brought supplies, mail, and passengers.

GAMAS functioned as an air ambulance and as a support vehicle for mission schools, Bible workers, and pastors. Many villages are not accessible by road; rivers often are interrupted by beautiful but dangerous waterfalls. These isolated villages can be reached in a relatively short time by air. The same distance would take many weeks to cover by foot or river. Through the work of the Holy Spirit and the efforts of faithful GAMAS volunteers, many people have found the peace that comes from knowing Jesus Christ as Lord and Savior. Jim

Gary Roberts preparing for a Guyana Adventist Medical Aviation Services (GAMAS) flight to a jungle village. These flights support pastors, Bible workers, mission schools, and other missionary activities—as well as serving as an air ambulance for medical emergencies.

and Lorraine Craik quickly determined that they wanted to be part of this work. "We would count it a privilege to share God's love here," they told Gary. "We'll return to begin working by the end of April two thousand five."

Gary and Wendy were planning to return temporarily to the United States for the birth of their first baby. Jim and Lorraine arrived in Guyana shortly before Gary and Wendy were due to leave. "I'd like to take you on this last flight before we leave to give you more experience in jungle flying," Gary told Jim, "but I'm loaded with supplies and already have one passenger. There just isn't room. However, there will be plenty of time for you to get your Guyana pilot's license and practice your jungle flying skills when we return after the baby comes."

That day, May 1, 2005, David Gates received a phone call from Bob Norton in Venezuela. "One of our planes has gone down in Guyana. I don't have much information." Praying earnestly, David began trying to call Georgetown, Guyana. After several attempts he finally made contact with Wendy.

"About one in the afternoon I got a phone call from one of the local commercial air services telling me to turn on my radio," Wendy told David. "The caller said, 'Paruima is calling and telling us that Gary is having trouble. The folks there want to talk to you.'"

Wendy had immediately switched to that frequency but could hear nothing. A Bible worker heard her on the radio and broke in to say, "Gary has gone down about a mile and a half from the runway at Paruima. People are now on their way to find him."

Wendy knew Gary was flying the Cessna182, a blue and white plane, and carrying one passenger. The next few minutes seemed like an eternity to her. With her heart beating wildly, she called the tower at Paruima. They hadn't heard from Gary for a while and had no indication he was down. All she could do was wait and pray.

Fifteen to twenty minutes later, Wendy received word that Gary and the passenger were alive but injured. As a nurse, questions raced through her mind: Was Gary conscious? What was the extent of his injuries? She was especially concerned

The wreckage of the Cessna 182 that Gary Roberts was flying on May 1, 2005. A strong downdraft caused the plane to crash as it was departing the Davis Indian Industrial College at Paruima, Guyana. Miraculously, both Gary and his passenger were alive, although injured.

about neck and/or spinal injuries. Would the Amerindians know how to move him properly? If he were conscious and his mind were clear, he could tell them how to move him.

As soon as Wendy knew that Gary and the passenger were alive, she called the tower. She asked for a flight to go to Paruima's tiny airstrip to evacuate her husband as soon as possible. Fortunately, one of Gary's good friends was flying near Kamarang, which was only a fifteen minute flight away. He had to wait a few minutes for the weather to clear. Quickly he canceled all his next flights to go get Gary and the injured passenger. Gary had crashed near the river, which made transport quicker and easier. Later Wendy learned that the crash occurred at 12:45 P.M. due to a strong downdraft on departure from Paruima, where the Davis Indian Industrial College is located. Nearly a dozen commercial aircraft had gone down in the same region during the time period GAMAS had been operating.

When Gary's friend landed at Paruima at 2:00 P.M., Gary and the passenger lay in a dugout canoe on the river below. Twenty minutes later, they were on board the rescue plane and heading for Georgetown. Gary was in a lot of pain. He thought his right arm was broken, possibly his left clavicle and his nose. Later Wendy made contact with the plane. The pilot informed her they suspected head and back injuries. He mentioned that he could hear either Gary or the other injured person making a crackling sound as he breathed with difficulty.

Wendy immediately called Dr. John Wilson, who had come to Davis Memorial Hospital in December. "I'll meet you at the airport," he promised, "and help you assess the situation and decide what to do with them." It was a long hour and forty minutes until the plane landed at Ogle Airport in Georgetown.

When Wendy first saw Gary at the airport, she thought two of his front teeth were missing; it turns out they were just covered with blood. The passenger had a laceration near his left eye but was unconscious. Gary said the man had been conscious and talking earlier. To the doctor, Gary seemed to be in more critical condition than the unconscious man.

Wendy felt especially grateful that Jim and Lorraine Craik were with her in this crisis. They had arrived in the country only the Tuesday before. Jim drove the van as they followed the ambulance. Although Gary felt miserable, his vital signs were good. The doctor, Wendy, Jim, and Lorraine felt that Gary needed a CT scan to make sure he had no head injuries, broken bones, or internal injuries. The bumpy road to the hospital was torture for Gary. Then, when they arrived at the hospital, they had to wait for the CT technician to arrive. In the meantime, the doctor started an IV and gave Gary a shot for pain relief.

Wendy felt so sorry for Gary; he had to lie perfectly still in a freezing cold room for two hours during the scans. When the test was complete, however, the news was good. Gary had no head, spine, or internal injuries. No bones were broken, though his extremely sore right arm had a big knot in the muscle. His right lung was 80 percent bruised, but it would not require a chest tube.

Meanwhile, Jim Craik went to the other hospital to check on Gary's passenger. His lacerations had been sewn up, and his injuries seemed to be confined to bruising and soreness, although X-rays would be ordered just to be sure. He was conscious now, resting and talking. Jim praised God for that.

Gary was taken to Davis Memorial Hospital in Georgetown. After the doctor sutured three lacerations on Gary's face and made sure he didn't need oxygen for breathing, he allowed Gary to go home. Fortunately, Gary and Wendy lived not far from the hospital. They brought an oxygen saturation machine to check the amount of oxygen in his blood. Both Gary and Wendy felt totally exhausted. Though Gary was in pain, they praised God that they could be together in their little home.

Did God work a miracle to save Gary's life and the life of his passenger? Can God preserve life when Satan tries to destroy it along with the mission airplane? Gary and Wendy are convinced that He can—and did—miraculously spare Gary's life.

Now the slow recovery process began. They could no longer fly to the United States, as planned, in the plane that now lay crumpled in the jungle. So, they placed their revised plans totally in God's hand and trusted Him to help them book flights on commercial planes a week or so later. They rested, relaxed, and looked forward to the birth of their baby, knowing that God had worked a miracle of love to save Gary's life. Recovery was difficult and painful, but Gary and Wendy were grateful for God's guidance and protection.

It took three different airlines for Gary and Wendy to travel to Washington State, but they made it in time to welcome their little son, Kaleb Seth, on June 4, 2005. All went well with Wendy and the baby.

June and July gave Gary time to regain his health; the pain lessened each day. In late July, Jeff Sutton brought the four-seat Mooney mission plane and flew the little family—Gary, Wendy, and Kaleb—to Guyana. The Mooney, a new addition to the fleet of planes owned by Gospel Ministries International, flies at 160 knots per hour, much faster than the Cessna 150.

Gary and Wendy are thankful to God for His miraculous blessings. Airplanes can be replaced, but not dedicated leaders and pilots.

CHAPTER 22

Miracle in the Jungle

Over and over God tells His children to "wait on the Lord" (see Psalms 27:14; 37:34). Sometimes we are told to wait patiently on the Lord. (see Psalm 37:7). In this way God helps us learn to depend on Him, but it can be very difficult at times.

Soon after they began serving as volunteers in Guyana Adventist Medical Aviation Services (GAMAS) in 2001, Gilbert and Melissa Sissons were finding it difficult to wait patiently on the Lord's leading. They saw so many needs all around them. The idea of assisting those in need in the isolated areas of a third world country is what drew them to volunteer as missionaries. God had prepared Melissa for this challenge through her training as a nurse in Loma Linda University and by her later work experience as an emergency-room nurse.

Gilbert and Melissa began working in the small village of Kimbia on the Berbice River in Guyana. Melissa was the only nurse for nearly a hundred miles along the river; she worked in a two-room clinic. Daily,

Gilbert and Melissa Sissons and their children. The Sissons began their volunteer mission work in the village of Kimbia on the Berbice River in Guyana. Melissa was the only nurse for nearly a hundred miles!

the situations she faced put her emergency-room experience to the test and increased her dependence on God immensely.

The most interesting part of her work came when she and Gilbert took their boat, equipped with a forty horsepower engine, and traveled the winding jungle river visiting outreach medical clinics. In May 2003 they stopped at the village of Wiruni twelve miles upriver from Kimbia Mission Academy. The hot, humid air offered no relief as Melissa assisted dozens of waiting patients. Late in the day, a young man approached with his little boy. The child was having pain in his ear.

Melissa noted the child's quiet, cooperative manner. He seemed to re-

The Sissonses' medical launch, the Good Samaritan, can travel the waterways of the jungles, supplying clinics and providing care for those who have little other access to medical services.

flect his father's gentle, shy manner. After treating the boy, Melissa asked, "Is there anything else I can do to help you?"

He smiled, held out his hand, and spoke simply and casually. "My name is Andy LaRose. I was born with a hole in my heart."

Intrigued, she placed her stethoscope on his chest. A harsh, whooshing, murmur vibrated into her ears. Surprised at the magnitude of what she was hearing, she asked, "Have you ever sought medical help?"

"Yes. I took a trip to a doctor in a nearby town. He put me in a public hospital for a long time. Then he gave me a note and told me to go home. The note read, " 'You have a heart problem and should stop eating rice.' That was all."

Melissa wondered what he had eaten for the last few years, since rice is a staple food in Guyana. But worse, the horrible truth hit her that Andy could have but a short time to live. She faced another unsolvable case in a country struggling to provide for the medical challenges of its people. She felt helpless. How could she help him with her limited cardiology skills and lack of appropriate resources?

Could God do the impossible and save this young father's life? Her faith reached up to the master Physician who had just planted a small seed in her mind that would soon blossom into a beautiful miracle. Six months of waiting and prayer passed. Then Dr. Tom Jutzy came to Kimbia to run a two-week dental clinic. At the last minute, his father also decided to travel with him. The pieces of Andy's medical puzzle began to fall into place as Tom introduced his father to Melissa.

"This is my dad, Dr. Roy Jutzy. He's a retired cardiologist from LLUMC."

Melissa's heart skipped a beat. "May I tell you about my daily prayer? Two years ago I met a young man, twenty-five years old and the father of three children. He lives in a quaint jungle home in a small village about twelve miles upriver. Everyday Andy ventures into the thick jungle to cut timber or hearts of palm, hoping to feed and clothe his family. Usually he can manage to work only a half day due to his increasing shortness of breath and lack of energy from his deteriorating heart. I'm sure that in a few years his heart will fail. He'll die a very premature death. Will you go and see him?"

"I'd be glad to go." Dr. Jutzy smiled. "Maybe this is why God impressed me to join my son on this trip. I know God cares for His hurting children."

Dr. Jutzy assessed and diagnosed Andy's problem and took compassion on his hopeless situation. He told Melissa, "Only heart surgery can repair the ventricular septal defect in his malformed heart. I promise you I'll try to find help for Andy. I believe in Loma Linda's untiring efforts mirrored in its core philosophy to help the less fortunate."

In the spring of 2004 the Sissons received the shocking but wonderful news that Loma Linda University Medical Center (LLUMC) had agreed to provide open-heart surgery at no cost to Andy. Dr. Jutzy, a man of his word, urged them to secure the needed paperwork for Andy to leave the country as soon as possible. For a year, Gilbert and Melissa tried to obtain Andy's birth certificate—without success. One problem was communicating with Andy due to his isolated location.

"How long must we wait on You, God?" Melissa prayed earnestly. "How are you going to make this happen? I know that You want Andy to have a new heart. Please guide us through this discouraging time."

Meanwhile, Gilbert began introducing Andy and his wife to God. They spent many hours studying the Scriptures together. Their eager minds accepted Jesus as their Friend and Savior. Andy also chose to accept each new truth in love for His newfound God. Gilbert and Andy prayed and meditated on the many promises in the Bible. Andy especially loved Luke 18:27, " 'The things which are impossible with men are possible with God.' " God used Andy's critical medical condition and the delay in obtaining the proper papers for him to go the United States for treatment to draw Andy's heart to Him. Andy's trust in God deepened.

Finally, time began to run out. In the spring of 2005 the Sissons were due to leave for the United States in just two weeks. If Andy didn't have his paperwork in order, this life-changing opportunity would be lost. Could God work a miracle?

Ask Melissa, Gilbert, and Andy.

They saw God open one door after another in a miraculous turn of events. In less than ten days Gilbert and Melissa were suddenly able to acquire Andy's birth certificate, his passport, and a visa for the United States! What an awesome God we serve!

When Andy arrived in California, the generosity of LLUMC proved to be a great blessing. The medical center provided accommodations and meals free of charge. The addition of Dr. Ramesh Bansal and Dr. Kenneth Jutzy to the team of physicians in charge of Andy's care made all preoperative testing smooth and worry free.

On April 5, 2005, the long wait was over, and Andy went to surgery. Led by Dr. Anees Razzouk, the surgeons were able to use the skills God had given them to transform Andy's malformed heart into a smoothly working one.

When Andy awakened in ICU, Melissa stood by his bed. She placed her stethoscope on his chest and heard a steady, even rhythm. *Lub-dub, Lub-dub, Lub-dub.* She removed the stethoscope and hung it back around her neck. Then she reached down and held Andy's warm hand. He opened his eyes and glanced at her. She saw a look of uncertainty cross his brow. He lay amidst the sounds and confusion of a busy hospital, far from his jungle home. He must have felt very lonely and afraid. Slowly he asked, "Am I OK?"

"Yes, Andy." Melissa gave him a reassuring smile. "You're fine, just fine. You have a new heart that is functioning perfectly."

Melissa felt a surge of joy in her own heart. The revelation of God's love bathed her soul in warmth. The impossible had just become a reality. Yes, God is a miracle-working God!

Andy returned to Guyana one month after his successful surgery. Due to sponsorship from Guyanese families living in the Loma Linda area, Andy could purchase his own chain saw on his return. He can now work full days cutting timber to provide for his family. God has revitalized his life and has given him many future years to work—not only for a living but to tell others of what God has done for him.

Extreme Faith

David Gates stared out the window of his study, seeing nothing. The challenges, the problems, the future, seemed overwhelming. It was not quite daylight, and he thought to himself, *Is the darkness before dawn like the dark clouds of debt?* Then, as he looked to the sky, he could see the first streaks of light. Slowly dawn changed the sky from blackness to pink and then gold. The heavenly drama replaced his mental turmoil with a great peace.

He picked up the open Bible in his lap and read the words God spoke to Joshua in Joshua 1:3. " 'Every place that the sole of your foot will tread upon I have given you, as I said to Moses.' " Then his eyes slipped to verse 5. " 'I will not leave you nor forsake you. Be strong and of good courage.' "

Thoughts of hope raced through David's brain. *How big a risk does God want us to take? Is it limited to the one and a half million dollars that we needed for the television station in Bolivia and which God so miraculously provided?* David recalled how the Holy Spirit spoke to one man who called just twenty-four hours before the deadline, offering to pay the remaining balance for the television network in Bolivia. Was it not God who had impressed three hundred evangelical pastors in Brazil to request that David go to Belo Horizonte, the third largest city in Brazil? Aloud he said, "Please, God, honor their request. Enable us to buy the station and broadcast in Portuguese as we've been doing in Spanish in Bolivia."

In his mind, David seemed to hear God asking more questions, *"Are not the five million homes that station could reach worth much more than*

191

one million dollars? Since the Seventh-day Adventist Church in Brazil has no television broadcast stations, wouldn't this be a wonderful opportunity to reach the masses? Shouldn't you also make that signal available to the eighty percent of the people in Brazil who have access to the Brazilian satellite? Will you not follow My command to go into all the world with the gospel?"

"But God," David spoke aloud, "what shall I do about the millions who live in São Paulo, the largest city in Brazil? And the millions in Rio de Janeiro? What shall we do about the TV stations that have been offered to us to purchase? What shall we do with the contract with satellite B-one which would give us access to thirty-four million potential viewers? God, You know it's a fabulous offer—a total of nineteen stations plus thirty new station licenses in new cities. Yet, how can we step out in faith and commit to give them a million-dollar down payment? How can we sign a contract for eighteen and a half million dollars when we have nothing? I don't want to fall into presumption, doing my will without Your leading. I know faith means prompt obedience to follow Your commands. I do trust Your leadership. But I dare not go forward without a direct command

The sprawling metropolis of São Paulo, second largest city in Brazil. The millions of people living in Brazil's major cities need to hear God's last-day message. God is as ready to work mission miracles today as He was in New Testament times.

from You. Help me to know."

Just then the door opened. Still sleepy, Becky smiled, "I didn't hear you get up. Then I heard you talking. Is everything all right?"

"Yes. God is opening doors at a pace far exceeding our human abilities. But no, everything is not all right as far as our lack of faith is concerned—faith to go through the doors God is opening."

Becky laid her hand on David's shoulder and bent over to kiss him. Then she sat down and asked, "Isn't that what you would expect God to do in these last days of earth's history? Doesn't God say that He will work not by human might or power but by His spirit? [Zechariah 4:6] That sounds like God's plans will be contrary to any human planning."

Becky got up and pulled a book from its place on the shelf. "I marked this quote the other day," she told her husband. "Listen:

> "God will use ways and means by which it will be seen that He is taking the reins in His own hands. The workers will be surprised by the simple means that He will use to bring about and perfect His work of righteousness.
>
> "Do not imagine that it will be possible to lay out plans for the future. Let God be acknowledged as standing at the helm at all times and under every circumstance. He will work by means that will be suitable, and will maintain, increase, and build up His own people" (Ellen G. White, *Last Day Events*, pp. 203, 204).

They sat in silence awhile, thinking. Becky broke their reverie. "Did you notice God said 'all times and under every circumstance'? 'All' is a mighty big word. Isn't He able to do whatever is necessary to make it possible for so many to hear the gospel?"

"I don't know what I would do without you," David told her. "When Satan brings discouragement and doubt, God uses you to remind me of His promises. I know that God makes Himself responsible for accomplishing His work."

"I believe God wants us to have a large faith in these days," Becky replied, "an extreme faith—that is, not just ordinary faith. After all, Jesus' faith in His Father while He was here on earth was a faith that stopped at nothing. That's extreme faith, and we should have the same kind of trust in Him, don't you think?"

"Yes. Jesus trusted His Father no matter the consequences. Jesus believed what God said and acted on it. I believe God can and will provide for *all* our needs. Jesus didn't know the outcome of His mission on earth, except by faith, but He went steadily forward trusting His Father. That's extreme faith!"

As His people step out in faith—extreme faith—God is honoring that kind of commitment. God's power is being displayed in amazing ways. Recently several Sunday-keeping pastors have led their entire churches into following God's Word due to what they have been hearing and seeing on the Adventist Spanish Televsion Network (ADVenir). Not only are these pastors and their churches keeping the Sabbath and following Jesus in their lifestyle, they are also dedicating their church buildings to their newfound faith.

In Colombia, where ADVenir is the only TV station in a certain city, 60 percent of the businessmen in that city got together. They decided, "We now know the Sabbath day is God's day of rest. Let's close our businesses, have a day off, and enjoy the blessings God promises to those who keep His day holy."

Cuzco, Peru, the gateway city to Machu Picchu, has fifty-six local national churches. Our manager reports viewers of all denominations stop him on the street and comment, "We thank you for ADVenir. What we hear is opening our minds to new ways of thinking about God. We're changing the way we understand salvation. Listening to ADVenir gives us new concepts; we believe that God will save us, not by our own works but by faith in Him."

Even though Satan tries to control the content of radio and TV, God uses them as a mighty tool to spread the gospel of salvation. The GMI team is working to add additional stations in thirty cities of Peru, including Lima. Those stations will reach the majority of the country. As the workers in Peru move forward, God provides for transmission equipment and installation costs.

In Santiago, Chile, a powerful TV station with national cable coverage reaching 80 percent of the country came up for sale. God helped the GMI team to make the first contact before competitors discovered the station was available. GMI reached an agreement on the price with the sellers and worked out a payment schedule. Surely God will provide for the cost of reaching Chile.

Even when God allows what seem to be setbacks, delays, and astounding challenges, He is giving His workers great opportunities to grow in faith. This is how Christians develop an extreme faith. What a privilege to experience His power!

God is opening networks right now to reach 18 million German-speaking people throughout Europe. This would be one of GMI's most expensive networks, and its success will require miracles, many of which have already begun.

In Romania, even with money in hand, GMI has experienced incredible difficulty trying to make connections so that the signal can be launched in that country. The Romanian Union is developing plans to maximize the network's impact.

In Asia, an evangelical pastor and his large congregation prayed and fasted for twenty-one days for a television network in order to reach the eighty million Telugu speakers in India. The Lord directed this pastor to the Internet, where he found GMI's Web site. After studying it intently, he contacted David and asked, "Would you be willing to partner with us? We could offer you six hours of programming a day for the network."

God continues to open more and more avenues to hasten His coming. Not long ago, He opened a door to developing an Adventist medical aviation service in Mongolia.

Presently, the only mission aviation program in Mongolia is Mission Aviation Fellowship (MAF). MAF invited GMI to work with them and also to share space in the only heated hangar in the country. Because of severe winters averaging minus forty degrees centigrade, the plane needed would have to be turbine powered. Beaver and Rebecca Eller, now in Mongolia, are making preparations for other teams. One family soon to go is Jeff and Fawna Sutton, who will head up the development of the medical aviation service in Mongolia. In this team of four are three registered nurses, two pilots, one mechanic, and one pastor, all dedicating themselves to volunteer mission service.

Gary Roberts, who now heads GMI's medical aviation work in Guyana, was born and reared in Kenya. He speaks fluent Swahili, French, another African dialect, and Indonesian. He recently completed a tour of the African continent to meet government leaders of different countries. God has blessed Gary's efforts with access to two aircraft for the English-speaking areas of east Africa—a twin-engine Piper Aztec and a Cessna 182. Gary and his wife, Wendy, and little son are making plans to move to the French-speaking part of east Africa.

Looking at all these opportunities and the challenges they represent in terms of resources—both human and financial, David says, "God seems to be saying to us, 'I know what you're trying to do for Me. I understand your human weakness. When you finally recognize your helplessness, I am ready to work. I have opened a door of opportunity for you that no one can shut.' "

David and Becky are convinced that God is ready to work miracles in our behalf to further His work—if we will place our hand of weakness in His hand of strength and exhibit an extreme faith in His leading.

CHAPTER 24

Modern Miracles

Recently David received a letter from Bob Norton, pilot for Adventist Medical Aviation (AMA) in Venezuela. As he read Bob's letter, David seemed to hear God say, "Tell the world this story. Tell them of a man who trusts Me, a man who has extreme faith. Show the world what happens when such a man commits his all in complete trust in my love and care."

Here is what Bob wrote:

I was in a hurry getting the plane ready for a flight to Ciudad Bolivar for maintenance. Emergency flights had detained me till late afternoon. I figured on three hours to fly to Ciudad Bolivar, for I had to stop in La Paraqua, plus a quick hop to the Santa Elena airstrip to pick up my passengers.

Thankful for fair weather, I made my way around big clouds. For about an hour I relaxed and enjoyed the flight in silence. I had turned off the radio because of noise and much talking, but suddenly I received a strong impression to turn it on. Faintly I heard my call, "AMA-AMA." Where was this call coming from?"

"Please take a patient to the hospital."

"What is wrong?"

"Man bitten very badly by a snake yesterday."

"Where are you? Describe the airstrip?"

"South of La Paraqua. Don't know how far. New airstrip about six hundred meters long. Been used at times, not often."

"I'll land at La Paraqua, leave off my wife and two other passengers, and do what I can to help you."

As soon as I landed, I asked other pilots for GPS coordinates. "Give me at least a heading and how far it is to Cuwaramapi."

One pilot raised his eyebrows. "Only two pilots go out there flying and never this late in the day. Don't even think about it." He shook his head.

"Why? How can I get there?" I asked.

"We don't have the GPS coordinates, but there is a pilot who does. He isn't here right now. What are you flying?"

I pointed, "That Cessna one-seventy-two over there."

"No pilot in his right mind would go this late in the day and never in that plane, trying to land on that airstrip. Why do you want to go?"

"I just got a call that a man was bitten yesterday by a poisonous snake. He's in bad shape."

"Is he an Indian or someone else?"

"I don't know, but what does it matter? It's all the same. He needs help soon, or he'll die."

"Probably he's just an Indian. Don't risk it! It's not worth it. The strip is only six hundred meters long, but the approach is up a valley between trees with a mountain on each side. You can't see the strip until you are too low and too far up the valley to turn around. A big mountain blocks that end too. As you turn short on final approach, between the trees, you'll see just a piece of the strip. That piece you see is about one hundred fifty meters long, and you'll be headed right into a bank. You must be almost stopped by the time that straight piece runs out because it turns eighty degrees to the left. Immediately it drops down over a hill. After that it goes up very steep to the far end. Why your plane might not even have enough power to get up to the far end to be able to take off again. Remember there are stumps, roots, and big ruts on the strip. It's very rough. No, you're crazy even to go near there."

I didn't like the report I heard, but I answered, "I feel I have to go to save a life. I know it's getting close to dark, but I must go to see how it is."

Resigned, they drew directions on a piece of paper. "This will help you find it," they explained. "Past this ridge you'll see a hump, then a river . . ." and so on.

With that, I decided to take off. Just then, a pilot ran toward me shouting, "Wait, the pilot with the GPS coordinates just arrived."

I quickly ran to him and asked, "Could you please give me the GPS coordinates for Cuwaramapi?"

His eyes got big as the other pilots told him what I was thinking of doing and the plane I flew. I pleaded, "Will any of you go with me?"

"No! Never!" they answered in unison. "Not at this time of day and not this late."

The pilot with the GPS motioned me to his plane, an AN2. He asked, "Have you landed at San Francisco?"

"Yes, quite often. That's a strip not worthy of the name airstrip."

"OK, this is how it is. You'll find a bad approach, worse than San Francisco. Hold close to the trees on the right side on short final approach to see the piece of strip better. That's where you must land. Only two of us pilots ever go near there, and only in the AN-two, a big Russian by-plane with a very short stopping distance. It has a thousand horsepower. Nothing like the Cessna you're flying, with only one hundred-fifty horsepower. I've never gone this late because you can't get back before dark. There is always a tail wind in the afternoon. It just can't be done!"

He sighed in resignation and added, "I know you are heading out there. Remember what I told you about the approach. You have to be very low between the trees before the turn, where you'll see the strip. Hold close to the right side."

I held out my hand, "Thanks a lot." Then I hurried to the plane and prayed, "God, please send Your angels to be with me. Help me not to try something that would hurt the plane. Keep me safe, so I can bring the man to the hospital."

With that, I was in the air. I followed the paper map waiting for the GPS to indicate I was close. I figured the time. If I could land and pick up the man, I would have just enough time to get in the air before dark. When the sun goes down this far south, there isn't any twilight. It gets dark immediately.

I got to the area and made a run at high speed as fast as the plane would go, hoping to have enough speed to get back out if need be. I didn't like what I saw.

Aloud, I said, "No, God, I can't land there."

I seemed to hear Him say, *"Yes, you can. I sent you here. I need you to land here."*

"I can't!" I argued. "There's nowhere to land. I've seen lots of bad strips, but nothing like this. I can't see anything to land on!"

"Am I not with you? Did I not call you to work for Me here? I need you to land and get that man out."

"OK, God, but only if *You* hold the plane in *Your* hands. I want *You* here, not just Your angels."

I heard Him say in my mind, *"I am right here with you."*

The radio came to life, and someone asked, "Are you going to land? Please help us."

I was circling high above and off to the side, not wanting to look again at that so-called strip that scared me. I answered, "Yes, have the man ready. We won't have long when I'm on the ground." I turned the radio off, for I didn't want any interference.

"OK, God, I'll go. But I must know You are here with me."

A great peace came over me. I knew God Himself was with me as I set up for the approach. A song came flooding into my mind, and I started to sing, "My God is an awesome God. He reigns from heaven above . . ." and then it trailed off as I dropped down between the trees. There was no tail wind! "Thank You, God," I whispered.

I was at fifty knots. *"Too fast,"* I heard in my head. I slowed down to forty-eight knots. Now, with full flaps, I knew I was so slow there was no way to go around again. I still couldn't see the strip. I slid the plane closer to the trees on the right side until they were just a few feet from the wing tip. I was still too fast. I slowed to forty-five knots and held that, adding power to keep from sinking. Now I was just two hundred feet from the end. Again I heard in my mind, *"You're still too fast."*

I wanted to add more power. But I knew that I would have to be as slow as possible to be able to get stopped before the corner, or I would hit the trees in front of me. Forty knots! Then thirty-eight! Fear filled me. Thirty-five—and we were on the ground.

Yes, I felt God guiding that plane; I know God was with me! I put the flaps up and hit the brakes hard. Then made a hard turn to the left. Praise God, we stopped!

I climbed out as two men came running toward the plane, carrying the patient between them. I looked at where I saw light. I saw where I had to go to get back off the ground. By then the patient and the nurse (yes, there was a nurse out there with him) had climbed into the plane. Would the plane make it to the other end of the runway? I rolled down the hill, then applied full power to try for the other side where I could turn around. I added all the power I had, praying, "God, push us up. If You don't help us make it on the turnaround at the top, the plane will fall on its tail. Then we'll be stuck there."

The plane just made it! I swung around and headed down the runway. Then I realized that if we weren't off the ground when the plane started back up the other side, it would cause damage. I put 30 percent flaps, forcing the plane off the ground. I felt it settle back on the uphill side and put the flaps back to 20 percent. Now the corner! At this speed on the ground, I would never be able to stay between the trees. As the ground flattened out, we were launched into the air. I dropped more flaps again to keep the plane flying. I banked steeply about 45 percent to stay over the strip between the trees. Then we were down the valley. We were into the air flying. Suddenly I realized there had been tree stumps, about eight inches in circumference, all along the strip that hadn't been removed. Also there were lots of roots and ruts. But nothing had touched the plane! I knew God had guided us through the maze of obstacles.

"Thank You again, God. You did it," I whispered, taking a couple of deep breaths. "Now I need You either to keep the sun up or make it possible for me to see in the dark. You know that when I get ready to land, there will be no runway lights on the strip—nothing to guide me on the approach, no lights to line up against the blackness."

In my mind I reviewed the trip back. I would be able to see the lights from La Paraqua. Looking down I would be able to see when I crossed the big river. Just before I crossed it to land, I would need to make an S-turn to stay away from a tall antenna. I remembered it stood near the runway.

"God," I prayed, "You have been a great flying Partner. Now please help me to see the runway as I cross the river and start the S curve, for I know there are no lights on the tall tower antenna. If You choose, please give me the ability to make out the silhouettes of a few planes parked on the ground."

And God did! Now where was I? Maybe in mid field? All I could see was blackness in front and below. As I started my downwind turn, I talked to God again. "Please help me to land safely. I can't see anything to give me reference."

I began counting in my head, *One thousand, two thousand* . . . Every few seconds I would glance at the stopwatch to make sure my count was right. Now left face. Still I couldn't see anything on the ground. I hoped I was over the strip. Then final approach! Descending at five hundred feet a minute with just a bit of extra air speed and holding my heading.

Again I pleaded, "Help me to see something!" Instantly I saw a straight line in the shadows and knew it was the runway. *But where does it start? Am I where I think I am?* Suddenly I saw flashlights waving back and forth on the ground. I could see them moving. *The people holding them must be running out of the hangars, so I'm fine.*

Then the lights of the plane picked up the trees, then the airstrip. Yes, just the right power back. We were on the ground! The flashlights motioned me over to a hangar. As the engine stopped, I opened the doors. Before I could get out of the plane, the other pilots had helped the patient out and put him in their truck. They were off to the hospital.

I poured out my heart in praise and thanksgiving. "Thank You, God, for being my God. Yes, You work miracles! You are all I need, my Master Pilot! You did it all! Thank You for working in and through me. What an awesome privilege to have You so close!"

We spent the night at the pastor's house before heading on in the morning. God opened many previously closed doors because of that flight. First, the news spread that I was willing to take such a risk for an Amerindian, that I considered them as much one of God's children as anyone else. The story of what God and I had done for this man soon spread throughout the whole area. God gave me and the rescue work we're doing, the respect of all—yes, even the skeptical pilots, the hospital attendants, and certainly the Amerindians! Now they know that our plane is their plane. They know we will do all we can to help them. Best of all, everyone in the area knows our God is an awesome God!

> I know that whatever God does,
> It shall be forever.
> Nothing can be added to it,
> And nothing taken from it.
> God does it, that men should fear before Him (Ecclesiastes 3:14).

Hating to see God get such glory, Satan increased his fiendish plans. Political convulsions rocked the entire country of Venezuela. The new president claimed that God gave him the power to clean up corruption and declared that certain missionaries must leave the country. News came that missionary aviation programs would be closed and their missionary families must leave. Rumors flew that the Adventist Medical Aviation program, serving the vast southeast region known as the Gran Sabana, must close. For years Bob Norton and his Venezuelan wife, nurse Neiba, had joyfully carried on their work of saving lives. The government set the date when all evangelical mission aviation programs, along with the missionaries, would be forced to leave. Municipal and village authorities had built a beautiful runway at Colgransa Boarding Academy in the village of Maurak. Would all this work come to an end?

The young village chief of Maurak sent word to all the villagers. "Only God can save our emergency medical flights. We have forgotten our spiritual heritage; we've not been faithful in our prayers. Tomorrow morning at five o'clock we request that all parents, children, airbase staff, teachers, and students fall to your knees in confession, repentance, and forgiveness. If we don't deviate to the right or to the left from all God commands us, He will hear our prayers to save AMA. Only His power can change the colonel's intentions when he arrives tomorrow to stop it all."

The village loud speakers came to life at 5:00 A.M. "The time has come for everyone to pray that God will demonstrate His power to reward and protect His work as He has promised."

Some hours later, a cloud of dust announced the arrival of several military vehicles. The colonel's face looked like an angry lion as he barked to his soldiers, "Videotape everything here. Call the missionaries." The village chief and elders crowded close.

Bob and Neiba Norton arrived. The colonel barely acknowledged their greeting as he announced, "I've come to close the aviation program. We will not allow an American aviation program to continue operating in our country."

A village elder respectfully interrupted him and quietly said, "My colonel, this aviation program is not American nor is it Amerindian."

"Then who's program is it?" demanded the colonel.

"This is God's program," responded the elder.

"Americans brought this religion, so it's an American program."

"No, my colonel. God Himself, not Americans, brought us the Adventist religion." The elders all nodded. He continued, "Long ago our ancestors received visions from heaven. An angel himself appeared to Auca, our chief, teaching him that we should worship on the Sabbath, eat only clean foods, and wear clothes. In vision they saw a great light come from this very mountain showing the place we should build our school. We believe our aviation program carries that light of God's love to all the Gran Sabana region."

The colonel looked confused and surprised, knowing the importance of indigenous religions in Venezuela. The elder continued, "So, you see our religion is not American but part of our native culture. Only God owns this aviation program, not Americans. They just help us carry out the vision that God gave so long ago."

Not wanting to get entangled in this sensitive issue, the colonel jumped into his vehicle and drove across the field to the boarding academy.

The Venezuelan principal extended his hand, "Welcome to Colgransa."

Ignoring the friendly gesture, the officer ordered, "Call all the students together. I've heard some disturbing things about this Indian school." The teachers quickly dismissed the students from classes and sent them to the cafeteria hall where all large meetings met. The colonel explained, "I've come to investigate rumors about the real mission of this school. One by one, I want each of you to tell me where you are from and why you chose to study here."

To his surprise, he discovered that the students had come from all over Venezuela to study there. That not all the students were Indians. His face began to soften, "You have a well-known, popular school hidden down here. We did not know this."

The fire gone from his eyes, the colonel returned to the airplane with his soldiers. "Mr. Norton, would you kindly take me for a ride, so I could see the school and the runway from the air. I'd like to take two of my officers too."

"I'd be glad to do so. However, due to contrary winds, I can take only one of you."

"I'm convinced you value safety as a pilot," the colonel remarked as the two of them climbed into the plane. The Indians smiled at each other, for they could see the tension from the angry military officer melting away. They knew who answered their prayers.

When the plane landed, the waiting people gathered around to hear every word the colonel said. He cleared his throat several times, obviously so choked up he could hardly talk. In a much more subdued manner, he said, "You have a wonderful program! You have saved many lives throughout the state of Bolivar. You must secure another plane and expand this program."

As they walked back to their village of Maurak, one Indian commented, "I'm excited how God answered our prayers. He protected our aviation program and school once again."

But Satan never gives up. Someone told the colonel's superior officer what he had done. In anger he exclaimed, "If he's not going to close the program, I will. Send word to Maurak village that in a few days I will come and will not fail. The government deadline will be met."

The loudspeakers came to life announcing the new crisis. The church elder reminded the villagers, "The same powerful God who intervened yesterday still rules. He said, 'Be anxious for nothing, but in everything by prayer and supplication, with thanksgiving, let your requests be made known to God' [Philippians 4:6]. Kneel with your families and plead with God."

Maurak's village chief called his council members together. Holding up a letter, he explained, "Our new governor is traveling around the state of Bolivar stopping at cities or larger communities. This announcement says he will visit our small village tomorrow. That's just before the general plans to arrive. Could this be God's plan to protect our aviation program from the general's threat?"

The governor went with the village chief and his counselors to see the plane and meet Bob Norton and his wife. His face reflected intense interest as he listened to the story of the medical flights and the many lives of his indigenous citizens they had saved. Showing him a card, Bob said, "This is a special security ID card from the previous governor's office. Word has come that this runway, built by municipal authorities and inaugurated with hundreds of representatives present, is facing closure. People plan to close it down, accusing us that this is a clandestine runway."

With a smile the governor turned to his assistant. "Please call the director of civil aviation." Then he turned to the villagers, "I can resolve this right away."

On the phone with the director, he asked, "Could you come personally to fix the paperwork on this runway, making sure it is correctly entered in the national list of approved runways?"

In a few days the director did just that. Within a week the governor made a second visit to the village to ensure that all had been done as he ordered. The general, very upset at hearing about the governor's visit and support for the runway, sent word he would soon come as planned. As yet, this has not happened. The aviation program is still operating; the mission plane is still carrying on its full-time work of saving lives. Truly God has protected His work.

But God did even more. First, He strengthened and enlarged the AMA program. Sufficient funds have come to purchase and refurbish a second aircraft, a Cessna 182 registered in Venezuela. This will double the area served. Second, Bob has received his Venezuelan citizenship since he is married to Neiba, a Venezuelan. Now he cannot be made to leave the country because he is from the United States.

God continues to take control of His work—not only in the isolated areas of Venezuela but in all the world. He bids His children, "Wait on the LORD" (Psalm 27:14). Many times to those who wait, the waiting time seems extremely long. During that time, not everyone will react favorably. Some will respond negatively. Criticism abounds. But no matter. The Lord " 'is the one who goes before you. He will be with you, He will not leave you nor forsake you; do not fear nor be dismayed' " (Deuteronomy. 31:8). If we believe that promise, we can know that God will teach us balance and provide us with tact, wisdom, and guidance, teaching us when and where to move forward.

The day of miracles is not past. If fact, the days of God's greatest miracles lie ahead as we near the time of Jesus' coming. Will we let Him use us, wherever we are and whatever our role, to work His miracles in and through us?

Want more mission stories? We've got them!

Mission Pilot
Eileen E. Lantry, with David and Becky Gates

The adventures of David Gates—aviator, nurse, computer specialist, and missionary—prove that there's no more exciting place on earth to be than in the will of God. David, and his wife, Becky, experience miracle after miracle in this modern-day story of mission service. This was the Gates' first book.

Paperback, 176 pages   0-8163-1870-0   US$12.99

Amazing True Mission Stories
James H. Zachary

From Africa to America, from the South Pacific islands to Siberia, miracles are taking place as God works to bring individuals to Himself. These stories will build your faith as you realize anew God's personal interest in our daily lives.

Paperback, 128 pages   0-8163-1982-0   US$9.99

More Amazing True Mission Stories
James H. and Jean Zachary

A second collection of remarkable mission stories from around the world. God still works miracles today. This follow-up to Zachary's first *Amazing True Mission Stories* proves it.

Paperback, 96 pages   0-8163-2079-9   US9.99

Order from your ABC by calling **1-800-765-6955**, or get online and shop our virtual store at **http//www.AdventistBookCenter.com.**
- Read a chapter from your favorite book
- Order online
- Sign up for email notices on new products

Prices subject to change without notice.